TOGAF 9
Foundation Exam
Study Guide

Kevin Lindley

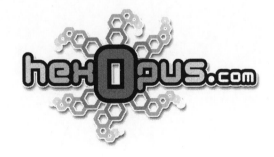

Page intentionally left blank

Dedication

Amanda, Anna & Gabrielle

.. .-.. .-.. . --. .. - .. -- .. -- .-. -- -. --- -. -.-. . -.. -... --- .-. .. ..- -. -.. ..- --

Page intentionally left blank

V10.8

ISBN: 978-1475054545

hexOpus Press

www.hexOpus.com

Page intentionally left blank

TABLE OF CONTENTS

Page intentionally left blank

This chapter covers the following exam subjects:

- The TOGAF certification program.
- Distinguishing between the levels of TOGAF certification.

CHAPTER 1

Introduction

There is a high demand for professionals in the information technology (IT) industry, particularly if you can demonstrate that you are a certified architect. You have made the right decision to pursue certification because being TOGAF certified will give you a distinct advantage in this highly-competitive market.

This Study Guide is intended to help you on your path towards becoming a TOGAF certified architect by providing you with the details you need to help your learn about TOGAF 9.1 and pass the TOGAF 9.1 Foundation Exam.

Audience for the Study Guide

This Study Guide is intended for students preparing for *The Open Group Architecture Framework (TOGAF)* Foundation Level 1 certification exam. It should also prove to be a useful introduction for students new to TOGAF or architectural frameworks in general.

What Does This Study Guide Cover?

Chapter 1	An introduction to the TOGAF certification program and general advice on preparing for, and taking, the TOGAF 9.1 Foundation Exam.
Chapter 2	The basic concepts of Enterprise Architecture and architectural frameworks.
Chapter 3	The core concepts of TOGAF, the ADM Phases and their purpose. Architecture Governance and how an Enterprise Architecture Capability can be established and maintained in an organisation.
Chapter 4	TOGAF contains a considerable amount of terminology that you should be familiar with: this chapter covers the terms that need to be understood for the exam and for subsequent chapters.
Chapter 5	The role of architecture views, viewpoints and stakeholders - and the relationships between them.
Chapter 6	An overview of the TOGAF Architecture Development Method, the Enterprise Continuum, Architecture Repository and Foundation Architectures.
Chapter 7	The Preliminary, Architectural Vision, Business Architecture, Information Systems Architecture and Technology Architecture Phases of the ADM.

Chapter 8	The Opportunities & Solutions, Migration Planning, Implementation Governance, Architecture Change Management and Requirements Management Phases of the ADM.
Chapter 9	The purpose of deliverables produced and consumed throughout the TOGAF ADM cycle.
Chapter 10	The ADM Guidelines & Techniques used to assist the development of the architecture covering business scenarios, gap analysis, risk management and capability-based planning.
Chapter 11	The concept of the Architecture Continuum, Solutions Continuum and how these fit into the overall Enterprise Continuum. The role of the Architecture Repository and the architectural artefacts it holds. Tool standardisation and tool selection are also covered.
Chapter 12	The concept of building blocks in relationship to the ADM cycle and details on both Architecture Building Blocks and Solution Building Blocks. Architecture Patterns and their relationship to building blocks.
Chapter 13	The role of the TOGAF Technical Reference Model (TRM) as a foundation architecture upon which other, more specific, architectures can be based.
Chapter 14	The role of the TOGAF Integrated Information Infrastructure Reference Model (III-RM) and the term *Boundaryless Information Flow™*.
Chapter 15	Architecture Governance in detail and the Architecture Governance Framework as well as the role of the Architecture Board and Architecture Contracts.

Chapter Overviews

Each chapter of this Study Guide contains some combination of the following materials:

Overview	Gives an introduction to the chapter so you can quickly see what will be covered.
Topics Sections	Covers the background information and the in-depth coverage you need for each exam objective.
Review Topics	Provides page references so you can review answers for each of the specific exam objectives.
Key Terms	Highlights the key terms used in the chapter.
Review Questions	Obviously, it is not possible to provide the questions that will be asked in the exam; however, the questions contained in this Study Guide will give you experience of the types of questions you will face in the exam. The questions are provided to help you identify the exam topics you have not yet mastered.

Further Reading and Resources	Provides further recommended sources of information for the areas covered by the chapter.

How to Use This Study Guide

Study each chapter carefully: make sure that you fully understand the information and the terminology used. When you are confident you know the material, take the test at the end of the chapter. Ensure that you can score at least 90% before moving on to the next chapter.

In order that you have a broad understanding of the subject area than just the information provided by this Study Guide, it is recommended that you review material referenced in the *Further Reading and Resources* section provided at the end of each chapter.

To learn all of the material covered in this book, you'll need to apply yourself regularly and with discipline. Try to set aside at least one hour a day to study in a comfortable and quiet place free from other distractions. If you work through this Study Guide, you will be surprised at how quickly you will learn the material and be ready to take the TOGAF 9.1 Foundation Exam.

TOGAF

TOGAF is important for the following reasons...

- It allows organisations to standardise on TOGAF as a methodology for Enterprise Architecture.
- It allows organisations to avoid lock-in to proprietary methods of major consultancy companies which can be very expensive in the longer term.
- It is an important step in making Enterprise Architecture a well-recognised discipline that supports the needs of the business.
- It provides rigour in the procurement of tools and services for Enterprise Architecture.

Why Become TOGAF Certified?

The reasons for becoming TOGAF 9.1 certified are:

- To demonstrate your commitment to Enterprise Architecture as a discipline.
- To confirm that you possess a body of core knowledge about TOGAF 9.1 as an open, industry standard framework and method for Enterprise Architecture.
- To allow you to establish a career as an enterprise architect.

TOGAF Certification Levels

There are two levels defined for TOGAF 9.1 people certification: Level 1 TOGAF 9.1 Foundation, and Level 2 TOGAF 9.1 Certified. Studying for TOGAF 9.1 Foundation can be used as a learning objective towards achieving TOGAF 9.1 Certified, as all the learning outcomes are required in both certifications.

The objective of **TOGAF 9.1 Level 1 - Foundation** is to validate that the candidate has gained sufficient knowledge of the terminology and basic concepts of TOGAF 9.1 and understands the core principles of Enterprise Architecture and TOGAF.

The objective of **TOGAF 9.1 Level 2 - Certified** is to validate that the candidate, in addition to knowledge and comprehension, has the ability to analyse and apply TOGAF knowledge.

For individuals who are already TOGAF 8 certified, *The Open Group* provides a certification path direct to level 2 (TOGAF 9.1 certified) known as the *Bridging Option*.

TOGAF 9 Level 1 (Foundation) Exam

The 11 topic areas covered by the TOGAF 9.1 Level 1 (Foundation) exam are **not** equally weighted. You should, therefore, concentrate on the key areas of ADM phases, the Enterprise Continuum & Tools, ADM Guidelines & Techniques and Architecture Governance. The list below shows the topics and the associated number of questions for each topic:

- Basic concepts (3 questions)
- Core concepts (3 questions)
- Introduction to the ADM (3 questions)
- **The Enterprise Continuum & Tools (4 questions)**
- **ADM Phases (9 questions)**
- **ADM Guidelines & Techniques (6 questions)**
- **Architecture Governance (4 questions)**
- Architecture views, viewpoints and stakeholders (2 questions)
- Building blocks (2 questions)
- ADM deliverables (2 questions)
- TOGAF reference models (2 questions)

The Foundation Exam is comprised of 40 simple multiple choice questions to be completed within 60 minutes. To pass the exam the candidate must answer 55% of the questions correctly. This Foundation Exam has no prerequisites and is a closed book exam. Passing the Foundation 9.1 Exam is a prerequisite for taking the TOGAF 9.1 Level 2 (Certified) Exam.

TOGAF 9 Level 2 (Certified) Exam

The TOGAF Level 2 (Certified) exam draws its questions from the following topic areas:

- ADM phases - Project establishment
- ADM phases - Architecture definition
- ADM phases - Transition planning
- ADM phases - Governance
- Adapting the ADM
- Architecture Content framework
- TOGAF reference models
- Architecture Capability framework

The Certified Exam consists of eight scenario questions, with gradient scoring, that need to be completed within 90 minutes. To pass the exam, the candidate must answer 60% of the questions correctly. Passing the Foundation Exam is a prerequisite to taking the Certified Exam. The Certified Exam is open book.

Any candidate failing an exam must wait for at least one month before retaking the exam.

Taking the Exam

The Open Group exams are run by *Thompson Prometric* and details of the scheduling of exams can be found on their website: www.prometric.com

As part of the testing process, you will normally be required to bring two forms of identification with you - one with your signature and one with a photograph. Normally, the author takes his passport and driving licence for any *Thompson Prometric* exam, but you should always check with the testing centre as to which forms of identification are acceptable a few days before to avoid any problems on the day.

Exam Tips

Arrive at least 20 minutes early for the exam to allow time for traffic or difficulties in parking: you can then use this time to go over any last-minute revision for areas.

The Foundation Exam is closed book so you will not be allowed to take anything with you into the testing area, but you will be given a blank sheet of paper and a pen. You should use the time before the exam starts to note anything down for areas you have a hard time remembering. It is a good idea to write down all of the phases of the ADM and the corresponding descriptions of these phases.

The Foundation Exam is only 60 minutes long, so use your time wisely and work through the questions methodically. If there is a question you cannot answer, leave it and come back later. The Foundation Exam has 40 questions so plan accordingly to make sure you don't run out of time and check your watch in the exam after every 10 questions to keep on track (10 questions = 15 minutes).

In the words of Douglas Adams "Don't Panic!". Just work through the exam methodically and diligently. There is enough time if you are prepared and the majority of questions straight forward and not designed to trick you.

Don't make assumptions or jump to conclusions. Make sure you read the questions thoroughly and all of the possible answers. Re-read the question to make sure you know what is being asked before answering.

For questions that you are not confident, mark them and come back to them later if you have time. Working through other questions will sometimes jog your memory and you will find an earlier question easier to answer later.

Use a process of elimination to remove obviously incorrect answers. This approach allows you to concentrate on the probable answers.

Don't leave any questions unanswered at the end of the test. There are no points deducted for a wrong answer, so answer all questions. Make an educated guess and you may just pick the correct answer.

Exam Preparation Tasks

Review All the Key Topics

Review the most important topics from this chapter. Table 1 below lists these key topics and where each is discussed.

Description	Page
Explain the TOGAF certification program.	3
Distinguish between the levels for TOGAF certification.	3

Table 1: *TOGAF certification exam syllabus checklist*

Understand the Definition of Key Terms

Define the following key terms from this chapter and check your answers:

- Foundation
- Certified
- Bridging Option

Complete the Review Questions

Check your understanding of this chapter by answering the following example exam-style questions:

Q1. How many certification levels are there in TOGAF 9?
(Select 1)

    A. 1
    B. 2
    C. 3
    D. 4

Q2. For individuals already TOGAF 8 certified, *The Open Group* provides a certification path direct to Level 2 (TOGAF 9 Certified) known as the _____ Option. (Select 1)

    A. Practitioners
    B. Transition
    C. Bridging
    D. Upgrade
    E. Conversion

Q3. Which of the following are listed by *The Open Group* as important reasons for TOGAF certification?
(Select 4)

    A. It allows organisations to standardise on TOGAF as the methodology for Enterprise Architecture.
    B. It provides rigour in the procurement of tools and services for Enterprise Architecture.
    C. It is the only certification program that demonstrates the candidate's ability to produce an Enterprise Architecture.
    D. It allows organisations to avoid lock-in to proprietary methods of major consultancy companies.
    E. It is an important step in making Enterprise Architecture a well-recognised discipline supporting the needs of the business.
    F. Individuals are entitled to become members of the *Association of Open Group Enterprise Architects* (AOGEA).

Q4. Which of these is a prerequisite for taking the TOGAF 9.1 Certified Exam?
(Select 1)

    A. Having passed the TOGAF 8 level 1 - Foundation Exam.
    B. Keeping an architectural journal for 2 years.
    C. Having passed the TOGAF 9 level 1 - Foundation Exam.
    D. Having passed the TOGAF 9 - Bridging Option Exam.
    E. Membership of the *Association of Open Group Enterprise Architects* (AOGEA).
    F. None of the above.

Q5. Which of the following are true statements about the TOGAF 9 Level 1 - Foundation Exam?
(Select 3)

    A. The exam consists entirely of multiple-choice questions.
    B. It is a closed-book exam.
    C. It has only 40 questions.
    D. It contains eight scenario questions and 40 short questions.
    E. It contains 50 questions that must be completed in one hour.
    F. All 11 topic areas are equally weighted and contain the same number of questions.
    G. The TOGAF Reference Models are not part of the Foundation Exam but are covered in the Certified Level Exam.

Review Your Answers

Review your answers by referring to the answers that can be found on page 180.

Further Reading and Resources

The following list provides further recommended sources of information for the areas covered by this chapter:

- The TOGAF website: www.togaf.info
- *The Open Group* TOGAF 9 Certification website: www.opengroup.org/togaf9/cert
- TOGAF 9 Foundation Datasheet, published by *The Open Group* - www.opengroup.org/togaf9/cert/docs/togaf9_foundation.pdf

This chapter covers the following exam subjects:

- The purpose and business benefits of having an Enterprise Architecture.
- What an Architecture Framework is.
- What TOGAF is, and what architecture is in the context of TOGAF.
- Why TOGAF is a suitable framework for an Enterprise Architecture.
- The different types of architecture that TOGAF deals with.
- The structure of TOGAF and a brief explanation of each of the parts.

Basic Concepts

The purpose of this chapter of the Study Guide is to introduce the basic concepts of TOGAF, Enterprise Architecture, Architecture Frameworks and the structure of TOGAF.

What is an Enterprise?

An enterprise is any collection of organisations that has a common set of goals, from a single department to a whole corporation encompassing all of its information and technology services, processes and infrastructure. In all cases, the Enterprise Architecture crosses multiple systems and multiple functional groups within the enterprise.

What is Architecture?

The ISO/IEC 42010:2007 terminology defines *Architecture* as:

> *The fundamental organisation of a system, embodied in its components, their relationships to each other and the environment and the principles governing its design and evolution.*

In TOGAF, *architecture* has two meanings depending upon the context:

1. A formal description of a system, or a detailed plan of the system at a component level, to guide its implementation.
2. The structure of components, their inter-relationships, the principles and guidelines governing their design and evolution over time.

What is an Architecture Framework?

An Architecture Framework describes a methodology for designing a target state for the enterprise in terms of a set of building blocks, and defines how these building blocks fit together.

The Architecture Framework should contain a set of tools, provide a common vocabulary, and include a list of recommended standards and compliant products that can be used to implement the building blocks. TOGAF is just one example of an Architecture Framework.

What is TOGAF?

The Open Group Architecture Framework (TOGAF) is an *Architecture Framework* and consists of a methodology and a set of supporting tools in the acceptance, production, use and maintenance of an Enterprise Architecture. TOGAF is based on an iterative process model supported by best practices and a reusable set of existing architecture assets.

The Purpose of an Enterprise Architecture

The purpose of an Enterprise Architecture is to optimise the existing processes into an integrated environment across the enterprise so that they are responsive to change and support the delivery of the business strategy.

An Enterprise Architecture provides a strategic context for the evolution of the IT system in response to the constantly changing needs of the business environment.

The Business Benefits of Having an Enterprise Architecture

The business benefits of having an Enterprise Architecture are:

Efficient IT operations:

- Reduced software development, support and maintenance costs.
- Improved portability of applications.
- Improved interoperability and easier management.
- Improved ability to address critical enterprise-wide issues.
- Ability to upgrade and exchange system components more easily.

Better return on existing investment with a reduced risk for future investment:

- Reduced IT infrastructure complexity.
- Maximum return on the existing IT infrastructure investment.
- The flexibility to build, buy, or outsource IT solutions.
- Reduced risk in new investment and reduced costs of IT ownership.

Faster, simpler and cheaper procurement:

- Buying decisions are simpler, because the information governing procurement is in a coherent plan.
- The procurement process is faster and more flexible, without sacrificing architectural coherence.
- Improve the ability to procure heterogeneous, multi-vendor, open systems to allow the integration of 'best-of-breed' applications.

TOGAF as a Framework for an Enterprise Architecture

TOGAF is a framework for Enterprise Architecture because it:

- Provides a platform to enable users to build open systems-based solutions to address their business issues and needs.
- Allows architectures to be developed that are consistent; reflect the needs of stakeholders; employ best practice; and give due consideration both to current requirements and the likely future needs of the business.
- Has been developed through the collaborative efforts of the world's leading IT customers and vendors and represents best practice in architecture development.
- Plays an important role in helping to improve comprehension and reduce risk in the architecture development process.

TOGAF and Different Types of Architectures

TOGAF supports the following four architecture domains as part of the overall *Enterprise Architecture*:

1. **Business Architecture** defines the business strategy, governance, organisation and key business processes.

10

2. **Data Architecture** describes the structure of an organisation's logical, physical data assets and data management resources.
3. **Application Architecture** provides a template for the individual application systems to be deployed, and for their interactions and relationships to the core business processes of the organisation.
4. **Technology Architecture** describes the logical software and hardware capabilities required to support the deployment of business, data and application services. The Technology Architecture covers the IT infrastructure, middle-ware, networks, communications, processing and standards.

TOGAF's Structure

TOGAF reflects the structure and content of an architecture capability within an enterprise, which is shown in figure 1 below:

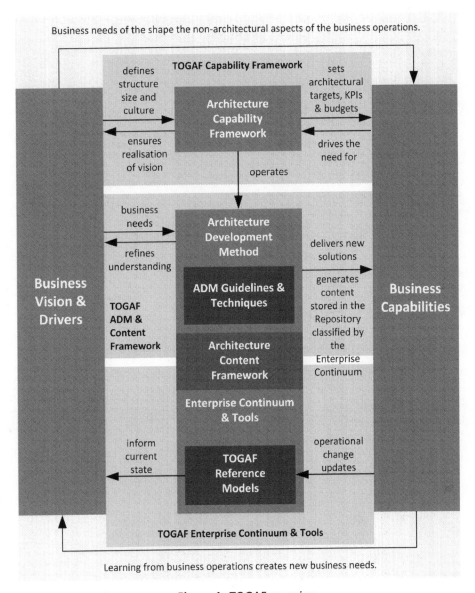

Figure 1: *TOGAF overview*

The TOGAF document consists of seven parts:

PART I - Introduction

Provides an overview of the TOGAF approach to developing an Enterprise Architecture. It contains the definitions of terms used throughout TOGAF and details changes from the previous version of TOGAF.

PART II - Architecture Development Method (ADM)

Describes the step-by-step approach to developing an Enterprise Architecture.

PART III - ADM Guidelines & Techniques

Provides a collection of Guidelines & Techniques for applying during the TOGAF ADM phases.

PART IV - Architecture Content Framework

Provides a model and overview of typical architectural work products, including deliverables, artefacts and reusable Architecture Building Blocks.

PART V - Enterprise Continuum & Tools

Discusses tools and taxonomies that can be used to categorise and store the outputs of architecture activity within an enterprise.

PART VI - TOGAF Reference Models

Provides a selection of architectural reference models, including the TOGAF Foundation Architecture and the Integrated Information Infrastructure Reference Model (III-RM).

PART VII - Architecture Capability Framework

Details on the processes, skills, roles and responsibilities required to establish and operate an architecture practice within an organisation.

Exam Preparation Tasks

Review All the Key Topics

The purpose of this chapter is to introduce you to the basic concepts of Enterprise Architecture and TOGAF. Please review the most important topics from this chapter listed in table 2 below:

Exam Syllabus checklist	Page
Describe what an Enterprise is.	9
Explain the purpose of an Enterprise Architecture.	10
List the business benefits of having an Enterprise Architecture.	10
Define what an Architecture Framework is.	9
Briefly explain what TOGAF is.	9
Explain what 'architecture' means in the context of TOGAF.	10
List the different types of architecture that TOGAF deals with.	11
Explain why TOGAF is suitable as a framework for Enterprise Architecture.	10
Describe the structure of TOGAF and briefly explain the contents of each of the parts.	11

Table 2: *Basic concepts exam syllabus checklist*

Understand the Definition of Key Terms

Ensure you can define all the following key terms from this chapter:

- Application Architecture
- Architecture Framework
- Business Architecture
- Data Architecture

- Enterprise
- Enterprise Architecture
- Technology Architecture
- TOGAF

Complete the Review Questions

Check your understanding of this chapter by answering the following example exam-style questions:

Q1. **Which of the following best defines an enterprise from a TOGAF perspective?**
(Select 1)

A. A collection of organisations.

B. A formal description of a system.

C. A collection of organisations with a common set of goals.

D. A group of individuals who share a common goal.

Q2. **Which statement best defines the purpose of an Enterprise Architecture?**
(Select 1)

A. To provide an application platform that enables users to build open systems-based solutions to address their business issues and needs.

B. To optimise the existing processes into an integrated environment across the enterprise so that they are responsive to change and supportive of the delivery of the business strategy.

C. To define a Data Architecture describing the structure of an organisation's logical and physical data assets, and data management resources.

D. To describe a methodology for designing a transition state for the enterprise in terms of a set of building blocks.

Q3. **In TOGAF, which of the following is not listed as business benefit of having an Enterprise Architecture?** **(Select 1)**

A. Better return on existing investment.

B. Increased customer satisfaction.

C. Reduced risk for future investment.

D. The ability to procure heterogeneous, multi-vendor open systems.

Q4. **Which of the following best defines an Architecture Framework?**
(Select 1)

A. A formal description of a system, or a detailed plan of the system at the component level, to guide its implementation.

B. A methodology for designing a target state for the enterprise in terms of a set of building blocks and defines how the building blocks fit together.

C. A step-by-step approach to developing an Enterprise Architecture.

D. An iterative process model supported by best practices and a reusable set of templates.

Q5. Which of the following **best** defines TOGAF?
(Select 1)

  A. TOGAF is an Architecture Framework, consisting of a methodology and set of supporting tools for assisting in the acceptance, production, use and maintenance of an Enterprise Architecture.

  B. TOGAF is a model and overview of typical architectural work products, including deliverables, artefacts and reusable Architecture Building Blocks.

  C. TOGAF is an Architectural Content Framework.

  D. TOGAF is a collection of tools and taxonomies that can be used to categorise and store the outputs of architecture activity within an enterprise.

Q6. In TOGAF, architecture, depending upon the context, is which of the following?
(Select 2)

  A. A formal description of a system, or a detailed plan of the system at component level, to guide its implementation.

  B. A methodology and set of supporting tools for assisting in the acceptance, production, use and maintenance of an Enterprise Architecture.

  C. An Integrated Information Infrastructure Reference Model (III-RM).

  D. The structure of components, their inter-relationships and the principles and guidelines governing their design and evolution over time.

Q7. TOGAF supports four Architecture Domains as part of the overall Enterprise Architecture: which of the following are part of this group of four?   (Select 2)

  A. Technology Architecture

  B. Business Process Architecture

  C. Governance Architecture

  D. Business Architecture

Q8. Which of the following make TOGAF a suitable framework for an Enterprise Architecture?
(Select 2)

  A. TOGAF has been developed through the collaborative efforts of the world's leading IT customers and vendors and represents best practice in architecture development.

  B. TOGAF provides ready-made solution architectures that are consistent, reflect the needs of stakeholders, employ best practice and give due consideration both to current requirements and to the likely future needs of the business.

  C. TOGAF plays an important role in helping to improve comprehension and reduce risk in the architecture development process.

  D. TOGAF can be used straight out of the box and does not need to be extended or established before it can be used in practice.

Q9. Which of the following are **major** components of the TOGAF document?
(Select 2)

  A. Architecture Content Framework.

  B. Continual service improvement.

  C. ADM Guidelines & Techniques.

  D. Architectural Execution Method.

Q10. **Which of the following <u>best</u> describes the Architecture Development Method (ADM)? (Select 1)**

    A.   The TOGAF ADM provides a model and overview of typical architectural work products, including deliverables, artefacts and reusable Architecture Building Blocks.

    B.   The TOGAF ADM discusses tools and taxonomies that can be used to categorise and store the outputs of architecture activity within an enterprise.

    C.   The TOGAF ADM is a selection of architectural reference models and includes the TOGAF Foundation Architecture and the Integrated Information Infrastructure Reference Model (III-RM).

    D.   The TOGAF ADM describes the step-by-step approach to developing an Enterprise Architecture.

Review Your Answers

Review your answers by referring to the answers that can be found on page 180.

Further Reading and Resources

The following list provides further recommended sources of information for the areas covered by this chapter:

- TOGAF 9 Part 1 - *Introduction*, Chapter 1 (Introduction)
- TOGAF 9 Part 1 - *Introduction*, Chapter 2 (Core Concepts)

This chapter covers the following exam subjects:

- The ADM Phases and the purpose of each phase.
- The deliverables, artefacts and building blocks contained in the Architectural Content Framework.
- The Enterprise Continuum.
- The Architecture Repository.
- How to establish and maintain an Enterprise Architecture Capability.
- How to establish an architecture capability as an operational entity.
- How to use TOGAF with other frameworks.
- The TOGAF document categorisation model.

CHAPTER 3

Core Concepts

The purpose of this chapter of the Study Guide is to ensure you understand and can explain the core concepts of TOGAF.

The ADM Phase Names and the Purpose of Each Phase

Figure 2 below shows the phases of the TOGAF ADM process:

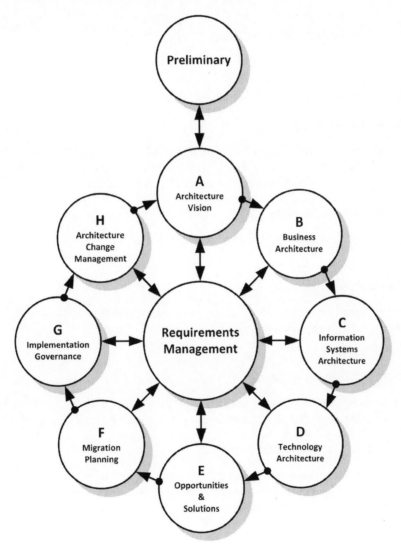

Figure 2: *TOGAF ADM overview*

The ADM phases are:

Preliminary Phase

Describes the preparation and initiation activities required to meet the business need for a new Enterprise Architecture. This includes the definition of an Organisation-Specific Architecture Framework and the definition of principles to be followed during the development of the architecture. This phase may include the customisation of TOGAF.

Phase A - Architecture Vision

Initial phase of the Architecture Development Method cycle includes defining the scope, identifying key stakeholders, obtaining approval and defining a high-level aspirational view of the Target Architecture.

Phase B - Business Architecture

Development of the Business Architecture consisting of a business strategy, governance, organisation, key business processes and interactions between them to support the agreed Architecture Vision defined in Phase A.

Phase C - Information Systems Architecture

Development of the Data Architecture (the enterprise's logical and physical data assets and data management resources) and the Application Architecture (the major logical groupings of applications that manage data objects to process data and support the business).

Phase D - Technology Architecture

Development of the logical software and hardware capabilities required to support the deployment of business, data and applications defined in the Information Systems Architecture Phase. This phase defines the IT infrastructure, middleware, networks and communications.

Phase E - Opportunities & Solutions

Initial planning of implementation projects for delivering the Target Architecture defined in previous phases.

Phase F - Migration Planning

Development of Transition Architectures with supporting implementation and migration plans in priority order. Activities include assessing the dependencies, costs and benefits of the various migration projects.

Phase G - Implementation Governance

Perform appropriate governance functions through architecture contracts while the system is being implemented and deployed to ensure compliance with the defined architecture(s).

Phase H - Architecture Change Management

Establish a change management process for the new architecture by continual monitoring of such things as new developments in technology and changes in the business environment to ensure that changes to the architecture are managed.

Requirements Management

Defines and manages a process whereby requirements for the Enterprise Architecture are identified, stored and controlled for use throughout the ADM Phases.

The Architecture Content Framework

During the production of an architecture that follows t[...]
produced such as architectural requirements, process[...]
structure called the TOGAF Architecture Content Fra[...]
placed. The TOGAF Architecture Content Framewor[...]
artefact or building block) to define architectural w[...]

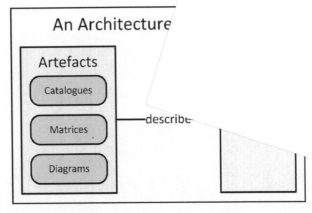

Figure 3: *Relationship between deliverables, artefacts and building blocks*

Definitions of the three architectural work products are:

1. A Deliverable

A deliverable is a contractual work product that will be reviewed, agreed on, and used for sign-off by stakeholders. Deliverables represent the documentation outputs of projects retained in the Architecture Repository for future reference as a model standard or point-in-time snapshot of the architectural landscape.

2. An Artefact

An artefact describes a specific architecture from a specific viewpoint. Examples of artefacts include use-cases, network diagrams and requirements lists. A deliverable may be made up of many artefacts. All artefacts should be stored in the Architecture Repository. Artefacts help to describe building blocks.

3. A Building Block

Building blocks are packages of functionality defined to meet business needs. Building blocks are potentially reusable and can be combined with other building blocks to deliver architectures and solutions. Building blocks can be defined at various levels of detail and can relate to both 'architectures' (Architecture Building Blocks) and 'solutions' (Solution Building Blocks).

The Enterprise Continuum

The Enterprise Continuum is a view of the Architecture Repository used for classifying architecture and solution artefacts as they evolve from generic (left-hand side of figure 4 on page 20) Foundation Architectures to Organisation-Specific Architectures (right-hand side of figure 4 on page 20).

The Enterprise Continuum allows generic artefacts to be leveraged and specialised in order to support the requirements of an individual organisation and comprises two complementary components - the Architecture Continuum and the Solutions Continuum.

Figure 4 on page 20 shows a pictorial view of the Enterprise Continuum:

19

rnal factors
ovide context.

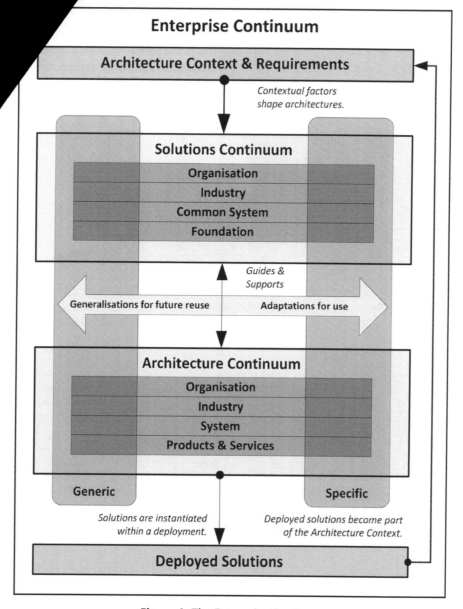

Figure 4: *The Enterprise Continuum*

The Architecture Repository

The Architecture Repository supports the Enterprise Continuum and stores different classes of architectural output at different levels of abstraction. An overview of the TOGAF Architecture Repository is shown in figure 5 on page 21.

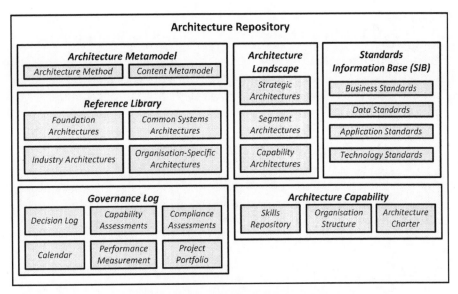

Figure 5: *The Architecture Repository*

The major components of the Architecture Repository are:

Architecture Metamodel

Defines a formal structure for architectural work products and artefacts to ensure consistency within the ADM and provides guidance for organisations that wish to implement their architecture within a tool.

Reference Library

Provides templates, patterns and guidelines that can be leveraged to create a new Enterprise Architecture.

Governance Log

Provides a formal record of the enterprise's governance activities.

Architecture Landscape

Shows an architectural view of the 'live' building blocks in use within the organisation. The landscape will be defined at multiple levels of granularity to suit different architecture objectives. Normally, three levels of granularity are defined - Strategic Architectures, Segmented Architectures and Capability Architectures.

Standards Information Base (SIB)

The Standards Information Base is a database of standards used to define the particular services and components of an organisation-specific architecture to which all new architectures must comply with. It is structured according to the services categories in the TOGAF Technical Reference Model and may include approved products, industry standards, services from suppliers or services already deployed in the organisation that can be leveraged.

Architecture Capability

Defines the parameters, structures and processes that support governance of the Architecture Repository to realise the business vision.

Establishing and Maintaining an Enterprise Architecture Capability

TOGAF provides an Architecture Capability Framework consisting of reference materials and guidelines for establishing an architecture function within an organisation. An overview of the Architecture Capability Framework is shown below in figure 6:

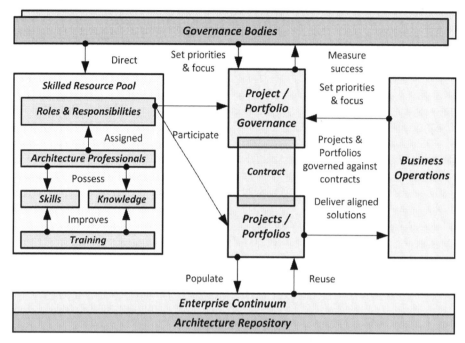

Figure 6: *The Architectural Capability Framework*

Establishing Architectural Capability as an Operational Entity

An Enterprise Architecture practice should establish capabilities so that it can be run in the same way as any other operational unit within the business, in such areas as:

- Financial management
- Communications
- Stakeholder management
- Risk management
- Resource management
- Performance management

- Service management
- Quality management
- Supplier management
- Configuration management
- Environment management

Architecture Governance

All architectural activity in the organisation should be controlled at an enterprise level and aligned within a single framework by Architecture Governance supported by an Architecture Governance Framework.

Architecture Governance Framework

The Architecture Governance Framework is integral to the Enterprise Continuum and manages all content relevant to the architecture itself and to Architecture Governance processes. The Architecture Governance Framework is generic and can be adapted to the existing governance environment of an enterprise.

Using TOGAF with other Frameworks

Any Enterprise Architecture Framework should provide:

- Definitions of the deliverables that need to be produced.
- A description of how they should be produced.

TOGAF is intended to be used in a wide variety of environments and does not prescribe a set of deliverables. TOGAF may be used either in its own right, with the generic deliverables that it describes; or these deliverables may be replaced by a more specific set, defined in any other framework.

Where custom deliverables are required, the architect will adapt the TOGAF ADM to define a tailored method and process for developing these deliverables. Guidelines for adapting the TOGAF ADM are defined within TOGAF itself.

Examples of other frameworks that can be used with TOGAF are ITIL, CMMI, COBIT, PRINCE2, PMBOK and MSP.

The TOGAF Document Categorisation Model

The model categorises the content of the TOGAF document according to the following four categories:

TOGAF Core

Fundamental concepts that form the essence of TOGAF (e.g., TOGAF core concepts).

TOGAF Mandated

Standard parts of the TOGAF specification and central to its usage; without them, the framework would not be recognised as TOGAF (e.g., TOGAF definitions).

TOGAF Recommended

A pool of resources specifically referenced in TOGAF as ways in which the TOGAF core and mandated processes can be accomplished (e.g., business scenarios).

TOGAF Supporting

Additional resources not referenced in the other three TOGAF categories, but which provide valuable assistance (e.g., release notes or evaluation criteria for tools).

Exam Preparation Tasks

Review All the Key Topics

The purpose of this chapter is to introduce the core concepts of TOGAF. Please review the most important topics from this chapter listed in table 3 on page 24:

Description	Page
The ADM Phases and the purpose of each phase (high-level).	17
The Architecture Content Framework: deliverables, artefacts and building blocks.	19
The Enterprise Continuum and how it classifies artefacts.	20
The Architecture Repository and its contents.	20
How to establish and maintain an Enterprise Architecture Capability.	22
Establishing Architecture Capability as an operational entity.	22
How to use TOGAF with other frameworks.	23

Table 3: *Core concepts exam syllabus checklist*

Understand the Definition of Key Terms

Ensure that you can define all of the following key terms used in this chapter:

- ADM
- Architectural change management
- Architecture Metamodel
- Architecture Capability
- Architecture Content Framework
- Architecture Governance
- Architecture Governance Framework
- Architecture Landscape
- Architecture Repository
- Architecture Vision
- Artefact
- Building block
- Business Architecture

- Deliverable
- Document categorisation model
- Enterprise Continuum
- Governance Log
- Implementation Governance
- Information Systems Architecture
- Migration Planning
- Opportunities & Solutions
- Preliminary Phase
- Reference Library
- Requirements Management
- Standards Information Base (SIB)
- Technology Architecture

Complete the Review Questions

Check your understanding of this chapter by answering the following example exam-style questions:

Q1. **Which of the following <u>best</u> defines the ADM Phase A?**
(Select 1)

A. Defining a process whereby requirements for the Enterprise Architecture are identified, stored and controlled for use through the ADM phases.

B. Establishing a change management process for the new architecture by continual monitoring of such things as new developments in technology and changes in the business environment to ensure that changes to the architecture are managed in a cohesive way.

C. The preparation and initiation activities required to meet the business directive for a new Enterprise Architecture, including the definition of an Organisation-Specific Architecture Framework and the definition of principles.

D. Defining the scope, identifying key stakeholders, obtaining approval and defining a high-level aspirational view of the target architecture.

Q2. Which of the following **best** defines the ADM Opportunities & Solutions Phase?
(Select 1)

A. Defining the scope, identifying key stakeholders, obtaining approval and defining a high-level aspirational view of the Target Architecture.

B. The preparation and initiation activities required to meet the business directive for a new Enterprise Architecture, including the definition of an Organisation-Specific Architecture Framework and the definition of principles.

C. Initial planning for delivering the architecture.

D. Development of Information Systems Architecture for an architecture project, including the development of the Data Architecture (the organisation's logical and physical data assets and data management resources) and the Application Architecture (the major logical groupings of applications that manage data objects to process data and support the business).

Q3. In which phase of the ADM would the organisation's logical and physical data assets and data management resources be described in a data architecture?   (Select 1)

A. Phase A
B. Phase B
C. Phase C
D. Phase D

Q4. Which of the following **best** defines Phase G of the ADM?
(Select 1)

A. The preparation and initiation activities required to meet the business directive for a new Enterprise Architecture, including the definition of an Organisation-Specific Architecture framework and the definition of principles.

B. Perform appropriate governance functions through Architecture Contracts while the system is being implemented and deployed to ensure compliance with the defined architecture(s).

C. Defining the scope, identifying key stakeholders, obtaining approval and defining a high-level aspirational view of the target architecture.

D. Development of Transition Architectures (defining Baseline and Target Architecture) with supporting implementation and migration plan in priority order. Activities include assessing the dependencies, costs and benefits of the various migration projects.

Q5. Which of the following **best** defines a deliverable architectural work product?
(Select 1)

A. A package of functionality defined to meet business needs.

B. A contractually-specified work product that will be reviewed, agreed on, and used for sign-off by stakeholders.

C. A description of an architecture from a specific viewpoint (e.g., use-case, network diagram or requirements list).

D. All of the above.

Q6. Which of the following are **not** architectural work products?
(Select 2)

A. A deliverable
B. The Standards Information Base
C. A building block
D. The Governance Log

Q7. Which of the following **best** defines the Enterprise Continuum?
(Select 1)

A. The development of Transition Architectures (defining current and Target Architecture) with supporting implementation and migration plan in priority order. Activities include assessing the dependencies, costs versus benefits of the various migration projects.

B. A view of the Architecture Repository that provides methods of classifying architecture and solution artefacts as they evolve from generic to specific. It allows generic artefacts to be leveraged and specialised in order to support the requirements of an individual organisation.

C. It is used to support the Architecture Repository and stores different classes of architectural output at different levels of abstraction.

D. A method for designing a target state of the enterprise in terms of a set of building blocks and defines how the building blocks fit together. It should contain a set of tools, provide a common vocabulary, and include a list of recommended standards and compliant products that can be used to implement the building blocks.

Q8. Which of the following are **major** components of the Architectural Repository?
(Select 2)

A. An architecture metamodel
B. The Enterprise Continuum
C. Projects / portfolio contract(s)
D. The Standards Information Base

Q9. Which of the following is a component of the Architecture Landscape?
(Select 1)

A. Business standards
B. Foundation Architectures
C. Content metamodel
D. Capability Architectures

Q10. Which of the following are components of the Standards Information Base (SIB)?
(Select 2)

A. Business standards
B. Foundation Architectures
C. Technology standards
D. Capability Architectures

Q11. Which of the following are components of the Governance Log?
(Select 2)

A. Business standards
B. Application standards
C. Capability assessments
D. Decision log

Q12. In which of the following does TOGAF recommend that an Enterprise Architecture practice should establish capabilities so that it can be run the same as any other operational unit within the business? (Select 2)

A. Supplier management
B. Licence management
C. Financial management
D. Industry standards management

Q13. Which of the following <u>best</u> supports Architecture Governance?
(Select 1)

    A. CMMI

    B. The Architecture Governance framework

    C. Service management

    D. The Architecture Repository

Q14. What are the two key elements of any Enterprise Architecture framework?
(Select 2)

    A. A statement of who will produce the deliverables.

    B. A plan of when the deliverables will be produced.

    C. Definitions of deliverables that need to be produced.

    D. A description of how they should be produced.

Q15. Which of the following frameworks can be used in conjunction with TOGAF?
(Select 1)

    A. ITIL & CMMI

    B. COBIT & PRINCE2

    C. PMBOK

    D. All of the above

Q16. Which of the following categories make up the TOGAF document categorisation model?
(Select 2)

    A. Core

    B. Draft

    C. Mandated

    D. Optional

Review Your Answers

Review your answers by referring to the answers that can be found on page 180.

Further Reading and Resources

The following list provides further recommended sources of information for the areas covered by this chapter:

- TOGAF 9 Part 1 - *Introduction*, Chapter 1 (Introduction)
- TOGAF 9 Part 1 - *Introduction*, Chapter 2 (Core Concepts)

This chapter covers the following exam subject:

- TOGAF definitions.

CHAPTER 4

TOGAF Definitions

The purpose of this section of the Study Guide is to ensure that you understand the terminology used in TOGAF.

Definitions

The following key TOGAF terms need to be defined and understood:

- Abstraction
- Activity
- Actor
- Application
- Application Architecture
- Application Platform
- Application Platform Interface (API)
- Architecture
- Architecture Building Block (ABB)
- Architecture Content Framework
- Architecture Continuum
- Architecture Development Method (ADM)
- Architecture Domain
- Architecture Framework
- Architecture Governance
- Architecture Principles
- Architecture View
- Architecture Vision
- Artefact
- Baseline Architecture
- Baseline Specifications
- Boundaryless Information Flow™
- Building Block
- Business Architecture
- Business Domain
- Business Function
- Business Governance
- Business Service
- Capability
- Concerns
- Constraint
- Data Architecture
- Deliverable
- Enterprise
- Enterprise Continuum
- Foundation Architecture
- Framework
- Gap
- Governance
- Information
- Information Technology (IT)
- Logical (Architecture)
- Metadata
- Metamodel
- Method
- Methodology
- Model
- Modelling
- Objective
- Organisation
- Physical
- Platform
- Principles
- Reference Model (RM)
- Repository
- Requirement
- Roadmap
- Segment Architecture
- Skills
- Solution Architecture
- Solution Building Block (SBB)

- Solution Continuum
- Stakeholder
- Standards Information Base (SIB)
- Strategic Architecture
- Target Architecture
- Technical Reference Model (TRM)

- Technology Architecture
- Transition Architecture
- View
- Viewpoint
- Work package

This section defines the key TOGAF terms and supporting terms that you need to be familiar with for the TOGAF Foundation Exam.

Abstraction

Abstraction is a technique of showing only those details relevant to the current perspective by hiding complexity that does not need to be shown.

Activity

An **activity** is task or collection of tasks that support the functions of an organisation; for example, a user entering a customer order into a sales system.

Actor

An **actor** is a person, organisation or system, which initiates or interacts with a system.

Application

An **application** is a deployed and operational IT system that supports business functions such as a payroll system. An application is separate from the technology components that underpin the system (such as the operating system it runs on).

Application Architecture

Application Architecture is a description of the capabilities that manage the data objects necessary to process and support the business.

Application Platform

An **application platform** is a collection of hardware and software components used to support an application.

Application Platform Interface (API)

An **application platform interface** specifies a complete interface between the application software and the underlying application platform across which all services are provided.

Architecture

The term **architecture** has two meanings in TOGAF depending on the context:

1. A formal description of a system, or a detailed plan of the system at the component level, to guide its implementation (source: ISO/IEC 42010:2007).
2. The structure of components, their inter-relationships, the principles and guidelines governing their design and evolution over time.

Architecture Building Block (ABB)

An **Architecture Building Block** is a constituent part of the architecture model that describes a single aspect / required capability and shapes the corresponding Solution Building Block(s) that will implement the capability.

Architecture Continuum

The **Architecture Continuum** is the part of the Enterprise Continuum comprising a repository of architectural elements. These architectures are developed across a continuum ranging from Foundation Architectures such as TOGAF, to Common Systems Architectures and Industry-Specific Architectures; to an organisation's own individual architecture.

Architecture Development Method (ADM)

The **Architecture Development Method** is the core of TOGAF and provides a step-by-step process for the development and use of an Enterprise Architecture.

Architecture Domain

There are four **architecture domains** within TOGAF:

1. **Business Architecture** defines the business strategy, governance, organisation and key business processes.
2. **Data Architecture** describes the structure of an organisation's logical data assets, physical data assets and data management resources.
3. **Application Architecture** provides a template for the individual application systems to be deployed.
4. **Technology Architecture** describes the logical software and hardware capabilities required to support the deployment of business, data and application services.

Architecture Content Framework

An **Architectural Content Framework** is a foundational structure, or set of structures, which can be used for developing a broad range of different architectures. TOGAF is an Architecture Framework.

Architecture Governance

Architecture Governance is the practice of managing and controlling architectures at an enterprise level and works in conjunction with corporate, technological and IT governance.

Architecture Principles

Architecture Principles define the underlying general rules and guidelines for the use and deployment of all IT resources and assets across the enterprise. Each architecture principle should be clearly related to the business objectives and key architecture drivers that they are to support.

Principles are general rules and guidelines intended to be enduring and seldom amended: they inform and support the way in which an organisation sets about fulfilling its mission. Principles are, essentially, a set of ideas that collectively define and guide the organisation from values through to actions and results.

Architecture View

An **architecture view** is a representation of a related set of concerns from a specific viewpoint. An architecture view may be represented by a model to demonstrate to stakeholders their areas of interest (viewpoint) in the architecture.

Architecture Vision

Architecture Vision has three different meanings in TOGAF depending upon the context:

1. A high-level, aspirational view of the Target Architecture.
2. A phase in the ADM that enables understanding and definition of the Architecture Vision.
3. A specific deliverable describing the Architecture Vision.

Artefact

An **artefact** is an architectural work product describing the architecture from a specific viewpoint.

Baseline Architecture

A **baseline architecture** is the system architecture before a cycle of architecture review and redesign - it can be thought of as the 'as-is' view.

Baseline Specifications

A **baseline specification** is one that has been formally reviewed and agreed upon. Any changes after the baseline version should be managed through a formal change control procedure.

Boundaryless Information Flow™

Boundaryless Information Flow is:

- A trademark of The Open Group.

- A representation of the desired state of the information infrastructure to support the business needs of the organisation through combining multiple sources of information and delivering secure information across the enterprise.

Building Block

A **building block** is a package of functionality defined to meet business needs. A building block is a potentially reusable component of business, IT, or architectural capability and can be combined with other building blocks to deliver architectures and solutions.

Building blocks can be defined at various levels of detail, depending on what stage of architecture development has been reached. Building blocks can relate to 'architectures' (Architectural Building Blocks) and to solutions (Solution Building Blocks).

Business Architecture

A **business architecture** is the part of an Enterprise Architecture related to the architectural organisation of business that covers the business strategy, governance, organisation and key business processes information, as well as the interaction between these concepts.

Business Domain

A **business domain** is a group of coherent business functions and activities.

Business Function

An identifiable component, which delivers business capabilities, aligned to the needs of the organisation, e.g., human resources administration.

Business Governance

Business governance is concerned with ensuring that the business processes, policies and their operation deliver the business outcomes and adhere to relevant business regulation.

Business Service

Business service is an explicitly-defined interface supporting business capabilities and governed by an organisation. For example, a business logic service may calculate or transform information and produce an 'output' (a function containing an algorithm).

Capability

Capability is the ability that an organisation, person or system possesses. Typically, capabilities are expressed in general and high-level terms and require a combination of organisation, people, processes and technology to achieve. Refer to page 105 for details on capability assessments.

Concerns

Concerns are the key interests that are important to the stakeholders in a system and determine the acceptability of the system. Concerns may cover any aspect of the system's functions, development and operation, as well as non-functional considerations such as performance, reliability and security.

Constraint

A **constraint** is an external factor that prevents the pursuit of a particular approach to meet its goals. For example, personal data may have to be stored and managed in the same country as the people about whom the data is held and not managed off-shore.

Data Architecture

Data Architecture is the structure of an organisation's logical and physical data assets and data management resources.

Deliverable

A **deliverable** is a contractual work product that will be reviewed, agreed on, and used for sign-off by stakeholders.

Enterprise

The **enterprise** is the highest-level description of an organisation and will often span multiple organisations.

Enterprise Continuum

An **Enterprise Continuum** is a 'virtual repository' of all the architecture assets - models, patterns, architecture descriptions and other artefacts - that exist within the enterprise and in the IT industry at large and which the enterprise has available to develop its architectures.

Foundation Architecture

A **Foundation Architecture** is an architecture of generic services and functions that provides a foundation upon which more specific architectures and architectural components can be built. The TOGAF Foundation Architecture includes a Technical Reference Model.

Framework

A **framework** is a structure for content and process used to provide consistency and completeness to a solution. An Enterprise Architecture Framework (EA framework) is an Architecture Content Framework that defines how to organise the structure and views associated with an Enterprise Architecture.

Gap

A **gap** is the difference between two states. A 'gap' is used in the context of gap analysis, where the difference between the Baseline Architecture and Target Architecture is identified and documented.

Governance

Governance is the discipline of monitoring, managing and steering to deliver the business outcomes required.

Information

Information is any communication, representation of facts, data or opinions, in any medium or form, including textual, numerical, graphic, cartographic, narrative or audio-visual forms.

Information Technology (IT)

Depending upon the context, **information technology** can mean:

- The life-cycle management of information and related technology used by an organisation.
- An umbrella term that includes all or some of the subject areas relating to the computer industry.
- A term commonly assigned to a department within an organisation tasked with provisioning some or all of the domains described above.

Alternate names commonly adopted include information services and information management.

Logical (Architecture)

Logical refers to an implementation-independent definition of the architecture, often grouping related physical entities according to their purpose and structure. For example, the products from multiple infrastructure software vendors can all be logically grouped as web application server platforms.

Metadata

Metadata is data about data. For example, the size of a text file is metadata about the text file.

Metamodel

The **metamodel** defines a formal structure for terms to ensure consistency within the ADM and also to provide guidance for organisations that wish to implement their architecture within an architecture tool.

Method

A **method** is a defined and repeatable approach to address a particular type of problem.

Methodology

A **methodology** is a collection of defined, repeatable steps to address a particular type of problem.

Model

A **model** is an abstract representation of a subject of interest. In Enterprise Architecture, the subject of interest is a whole or part of the enterprise and the model is used to construct 'views' that address the concerns of particular stakeholders.

Modelling

Modelling is a technique that uses models to represent a subject in a form. This allows easier reasoning, insight and clarity concerning the essence of the subject matter, without dealing with the subject directly.

Objective

An **objective** is a time-bounded milestone for an organisation used to demonstrate progress towards a goal; for example, 'increase market share by 30% by the end of 2015'.

Organisation

An **organisation** is a self-contained unit of resources with a defined responsibly, goals, objectives and measures.

Physical

Physical is a description of a real-world entity.

Platform

A **platform** is a combination of technology products and components used to host application software.

Principles

Principles are general rules and guidelines intended to define the use and deployment of resources and assets across the enterprise.

Reference Model (RM)

A **reference model** is an abstract framework for:

- understanding relationships between entities of an environment.
- developing consistent standards or specifications supporting that environment.

A reference model may be used as a basis for education and explaining standards to a non-specialist.

Repository

A **repository** is a system that manages all of an enterprise's data including process models and other enterprise information.

Requirement

A **requirement** is a quantitative statement of business need that must be met by a particular architecture or work package.

Roadmap

A **roadmap** is an abstract plan for business or technology change.

Segment Architecture

Segment architecture is a formal and detailed description of areas within an organisation used at the programme level.

Skill

A **skill** is the ability to perform a job-specific activity.

Solution Architecture

Solution Architecture is a description of a business operation or activity and how it supports that operation. Solution Architecture typically applies to a single project or project release, assisting in the translation of requirements into a solution vision, high-level business and/or IT system specifications as well as a portfolio of implementation tasks.

Solution Building Block (SBB)

A **Solution Building Block** is a physical solution for an Architecture Building Block.

Solutions Continuum

The **Solutions Continuum** is part of the Enterprise Continuum representing a repository of reusable solutions that can be used for future implementations.

Stakeholder

A **stakeholder** is an individual, team or organisation with interests in the outcome of the architecture.

Standards Information Base (SIB)

The **Standards Information Base** is a database of standards used to define the particular services and components of an Organisation-Specific Architecture to which all new architectures must comply with. It is structured according to the services categories in the TOGAF Technical Reference Model and may include approved products, industry standards, services from suppliers or services already deployed in the organisation that can be leveraged.

Strategic Architecture

Strategic Architecture is a formal description of the enterprise, providing an organising framework for operational and change activity. A strategic architecture can also be used as an executive-level, long-term view for direction setting.

Target Architecture

Target Architecture is a description of a future state of the architecture. There may be several future states developed as a roadmap to show the evolution of the architecture to a target state - these are called Transition Architectures.

Technology Architecture

Technology Architecture is the logical software and hardware capabilities required to support deployment of business, data and application services. This includes IT infrastructure, middleware, networks, communications, processing and standards.

Technical Reference Model (TRM)

The **Technical Reference Model** is a structure for describing the components of an information system and provides a model and taxonomy of generic platform services.

Transition Architecture

Transition Architecture is a formal description of the Enterprise Architecture showing periods of transition and development for particular parts of the enterprise. Transition Architectures are used to provide an overview of current and target capability, and to allow for individual work packages and projects to be grouped into managed portfolios and programmes. Refer to page 108 for details on Transition Architecture.

View

A **view** is the representation of a related set of concerns. A view is what is seen from a viewpoint. An architecture view may be represented by a model to demonstrate to stakeholders their areas of interest in the architecture. A view does not have to be visual or graphical in nature, although many of them are.

Viewpoint

A **viewpoint** is a definition of the perspective from which a view is taken. A view is what you see; a viewpoint is where you are looking from or a perspective that determines what you see.

Work Package

A **work package** is a set of actions used to achieve one or more business objectives.

Exam Preparation Tasks

Review All the Key Topics

The purpose of this chapter is to introduce the definitions used in TOGAF. Please review the most important topics from this chapter listed in Table 4 below:

Description	Page
You must be able to understand and explain the definitions of the key terms defined in this chapter.	29-36

Table 4: *General definitions exam syllabus checklist*

Understand the Definition of Key Terms

Define the following key terms from this chapter, and check your answers with the definitions given earlier in this chapter:

- Abstraction
- Activity
- Actor
- Application
- Application Architecture
- Application Platform
- Application Platform Interface
- Architecture
- Architecture Building Block
- Architecture Continuum
- Architecture Development Method
- Architecture Domain
- Architecture Content Framework
- Architecture Governance
- Architecture Principles
- Architecture View
- Architecture Vision
- Artefact
- Baseline Architecture
- Baseline Specifications
- Boundaryless Information Flow™
- Business Architecture
- Business Domain
- Business Function
- Business Governance
- Business Service
- Capability
- Concerns
- Constraint
- Data Architecture
- Deliverable
- Enterprise Continuum

- Foundation Architecture
- Framework
- Gap
- Information
- Information Technology (IT)
- Logical (Architecture)
- Metadata
- Metamodel
- Method / Methodology
- Model / Modelling
- Objective
- Organisation
- Physical
- Platform
- Principles
- Reference Model (RM)
- Repository
- Requirement
- Roadmap
- Segment Architecture
- Solution Architecture
- Solution Building Block
- Solution Continuum
- Stakeholder
- Standards Information Base
- Strategic Architecture
- Target Architecture
- Technology Architecture
- Technical Reference Model
- Transition Architecture
- Viewpoint
- Work Package

Complete the Review Questions

Check your understanding of this chapter by answering the following example exam-style questions:

Q1. **Which of the following <u>best</u> defines an activity?**
(Select 1)

  A. A time-bounded milestone for an organisation used to demonstrate progress towards a goal.

  B. A representation of a related set of concerns from a specific viewpoint. It may be represented by a model to demonstrate to stakeholders their areas of interest (viewpoint) in the architecture.

  C. A defined, repeatable approach to address a particular type of problem.

  D. A task or collection of tasks that support the functions of an organisation.

Q2. **Which of the following <u>best</u> defines an application?**
(Select 1)

  A. A possible physical solution for an Architecture Building Block.

  B. A deployed and operational IT system that supports business functions such as a payroll system but separate from the technology components that underpin the system.

  C. A formal description of the Enterprise Architecture showing periods of transition and development for particular parts of the enterprise.

  D. An implementation-independent definition of the architecture, often grouping related physical entities according to their purpose and structure.

Q3. **Which of the following <u>best</u> defines an Application Architecture?**
(Select 1)

  A. The structure of components, their inter-relationships and the principles and guidelines governing their design and evolution over time.

  B. A formal description of the Enterprise Architecture showing periods of transition and development for particular parts of the enterprise.

  C. A possible physical solution for an Architecture Building Block.

  D. A description of the capabilities that manage the data objects necessary to process and support the business.

Q4. **Which of the following <u>best</u> defines an Architecture Building Block?**
(Select 1)

  A. A single aspect / required capability that shapes the corresponding Solution Building Block or blocks that will implement the capability.

  B. The structure of components, their inter-relationships, and the principles and guidelines governing their design and evolution over time.

  C. A candidate physical solution for a Solution Building Block.

  D. A constituent part of the architecture model that describes a single aspect / required capability and shapes the corresponding Solution Building Block(s) that will implement the capability.

Q5. Which of the following **best** defines the Architecture Development Method?
(Select 1)

A. A discipline of monitoring, managing and steering a business to deliver the required outcomes.

B. A step-by-step process for the development and use of an Enterprise Architecture.

C. A system that manages all of the data of an enterprise, including data and process models and other enterprise information.

D. A technique that, by the construction of models, enables a subject to be represented in a form that allows reasoning, insight and clarity concerning the essence of the subject matter.

Q6. Which of the following are architecture domains within TOGAF?
(Select 2)

A. System architecture

B. Component architecture

C. Business Architecture

D. Data Architecture

Q7. Which of the following **best** defines an Architecture Framework?
(Select 1)

A. A foundation structure, or set of structures, which can be used to develop a broad range of different architectures.

B. A structure concerned with ensuring that the business processes, policies and their operation deliver the business outcomes and adheres to relevant business regulation.

C. The representation of a related set of concerns.

D. A formal description of the Enterprise Architecture showing periods of transition and development for particular parts of the enterprise.

Q8. Which of the following **best** defines Architecture Principles?
(Select 1)

A. The core of TOGAF, providing a step-by-step process for the development and use of an Enterprise Architecture.

B. An abstract framework for understanding significant relationships among the entities of an environment.

C. A process for ensuring that the business processes, policies and their operation deliver the business outcomes and adhere to relevant business regulation.

D. The underlying general rules and guidelines for the use and deployment of all IT resources and assets across the enterprise.

Q9. Which of the following **best** defines an architecture view?
(Select 1)

A. An overview of current and target capability that allows for individual work packages and projects to be grouped into managed portfolios and programmes.

B. A representation of a related set of concerns from a specific viewpoint.

C. A high-level, aspirational view of the target architecture.

D. A technique that, by the construction of models, enables a subject to be represented in a form that allows reasoning, insight and clarity concerning the essence of the subject matter.

Q10. **Which different meanings of the term Architecture Vision are used in TOGAF?**
(Select 2)

    A.   A high-level, aspirational view of the Target Architecture.

    B.   A representation of a related set of concerns from a specific viewpoint.

    C.   A phase in the ADM that delivers understanding and definition of the Target Architecture.

    D.   A formal description of the Enterprise Architecture showing periods of transition and development for particular parts of the enterprise.

Q11. **Which of the following <u>best</u> defines a Baseline Specification?**
(Select 1)

    A.   A formal description of the Enterprise Architecture showing periods of transition and development for particular parts of the enterprise.

    B.   A time-bounded milestone for an organisation used to demonstrate progress towards a goal.

    C.   A specification that has been formally reviewed and agreed upon.

    D.   The system architecture before a cycle of architecture review and redesign - it can be thought of as the 'as-is' view.

Q12. **Which of the following <u>best</u> defines Baseline Architecture?**
(Select 1)

    A.   A formal description of the enterprise, providing an organising framework for operational and change activity and an executive-level, long-term view for direction setting.

    B.   The system architecture before a cycle of architecture review and redesign - it can be thought of as the 'as-is' view.

    C.   A formal description of the Enterprise Architecture showing periods of transition and development for particular parts of the enterprise.

    D.   A phase in the ADM that delivers understanding and definition of the Architecture Vision.

Q13. **Which of the following <u>best</u> defines a building block?**
(Select 1)

    A.   A package of functionality defined to meet business needs.

    B.   A formal description of the Enterprise Architecture showing periods of transition and development for particular parts of the enterprise.

    C.   A phase in the ADM that delivers understanding and definition of the Architecture Vision.

    D.   A System Architecture before a cycle of architecture review and redesign - it can be thought of as the 'as-is' view.

Q14. **Which of the following <u>best</u> defines Business Architecture?**
(Select 1)

    A.   A formal description of the Enterprise Architecture showing periods of transition and development for particular parts of the enterprise.

    B.   Logical software and hardware capabilities that are required to support the deployment of business, data and application services.

    C.   A formal, summary description of the enterprise, providing an organising framework for operational and change activity and an executive-level, long-term view for direction setting.

    D.   Part of an Enterprise Architecture related to the architectural organisation of business that covers the business strategy, governance, organisation and key business processes information, as well as the interaction between these concepts.

Q15. Which of the following <u>best</u> defines business governance?
(Select 1)

    A.   A formal, summary description of the enterprise, providing an organising framework for operational and change activity and an executive-level, long-term view for direction setting.

    B.   Ensuring that the business processes, policies and their operation deliver the business outcomes and adhere to relevant business regulation.

    C.   Part of an Enterprise Architecture related to the architectural organisation of business that covers the business strategy, governance, organisation and key business processes information, as well as the interaction between these concepts.

    D.   A defined, repeatable series of steps to address a particular type of problem.

Q16. Which of the following <u>best</u> defines a capability?
(Select 1)

    A.   The representation of a related set of concerns.

    B.   Ensuring that the business processes, policies and their operation deliver the business outcomes and adhere to relevant business regulation.

    C.   A defined, repeatable series of steps to address a particular type of problem.

    D.   The ability that an organisation, person or system possesses.

Q17. Which of the following <u>best</u> defines an architectural concern?
(Select 1)

    A.   A definition of the perspective from which a view is taken.

    B.   The ability that an organisation, person, or system possesses.

    C.   A quantitative statement of business need that must be met by a particular architecture or work package.

    D.   The key interest that is important to the stakeholders in a system and determines the acceptability of the system.

Q18. Which of the following <u>best</u> defines a constraint?
(Select 1)

    A.   The key interest that is important to the stakeholders in a system and determines the acceptability of the system.

    B.   An external factor that prevents the pursuit of particular approach to meet its goals.

    C.   A quantitative statement of business need that must be met by a particular architecture or work package.

    D.   A time-bounded milestone for an organisation used to demonstrate progress towards a goal.

Q19. Which of the following <u>best</u> defines Data Architecture?
(Select 1)

    A.   A formal description of the enterprise, providing an organising framework for operational and change activity and an executive-level, long-term view for direction setting.

    B.   The logical software and hardware capabilities required to support the deployment of business, data and application services.

    C.   The structure of an organisation's logical and physical data assets and data management resources.

    D.   A description of a future state of the architecture being developed for an organisation.

Q20. **Which of the following best defines a deliverable in TOGAF?**
(Select 1)

A. An architectural work product that is contractually specified, formally reviewed, agreed upon, and signed off by stakeholders.

B. A time-bounded milestone for an organisation used to demonstrate progress towards a goal.

C. A quantitative statement of business need that must be met by a particular architecture or work package.

D. A representation of a subject of interest that provides an abstract representation of the subject.

Q21. **Which of the following best defines an enterprise in TOGAF?**
(Select 1)

A. The highest-level description of an organisation (and typically covers all missions and functions). It will often span multiple organisations.

B. A formal description of the enterprise, providing an organising framework for operational and change activity and an executive-level, long-term view for direction setting.

C. An abstract framework for understanding significant relationships among the entities of an environment and for the development of consistent standards or specifications supporting that environment.

D. A constituent part of the architecture model that describes a single aspect / required capability and shapes the corresponding Solution Building Block(s) that will implement the capability.

Q22. **Which of the following best defines a Foundation Architecture?**
(Select 1)

A. A description of a discrete business operation or activity and how IT supports that operation.

B. The logical software and hardware capabilities required to support deployment of business, data and application services.

C. An architecture of generic services and functions upon which more specific architectures and architectural components can be built.

D. The part of an Enterprise Architecture related to architectural organisation of business that covers the business strategy, governance, organisation and key business processes information, as well as the interaction between these concepts.

Q23. **Which of the following best defines a gap?**
(Select 1)

A. The perspective from which a view is taken.

B. A quantitative statement of business need that must be met by a particular architecture or work package.

C. A representation of a subject of interest that provides an abstract representation of the subject.

D. The difference between two states.

Q24. **Which of the following best defines governance?**
(Select 1)

A. The core of TOGAF providing a step-by-step process for the development and use of an Enterprise Architecture.

B. The discipline of monitoring, managing and steering a business to deliver the outcomes required.

C. Ensuring that the business processes, policies and their operation deliver the business outcomes and adhere to relevant business regulations.

D. The underlying general rules and guidelines for the use and deployment of all IT resources and assets across the enterprise.

Q25. Which of the following <u>best</u> defines the term information?
(Select 1)

A. A system that manages all of the data of an enterprise, including, and process models and other enterprise information.

B. Any communication or representation of facts, data or opinions in any medium or form, including textual, numerical, graphic, cartographic, narrative or audio-visual forms.

C. A formal structure for terms to ensure there is consistency within the ADM, and also to provide guidance for organisations that wish to implement their architecture within an architecture tool.

D. A quantitative statement of business need that must be met by a particular architecture or work package.

Q26. Depending upon the context, information technology can mean which of the following?
(Select 2)

A. The life-cycle management of information and related technology used by an organisation.

B. A defined, repeatable series of steps to address a particular type of problem.

C. A candidate-logical solution for a Solution Building Block.

D. An umbrella term that includes all or some of the subject areas relating to the computer industry.

Q27. Which of the following <u>best</u> defines the term logical (architecture)?
(Select 1)

A. A description of a real-world entity.

B. An abstract framework for understanding significant relationships among the entities of an environment and for the development of consistent standards or specifications supporting that environment.

C. An implementation-independent definition of the architecture, often grouping related physical entities according to their purpose and structure.

D. An architectural work product that is contractually specified, formally reviewed, agreed upon, and signed off by stakeholders.

Q28. Which of the following <u>best</u> defines the term metadata?
(Select 1)

A. Data about data.

B. A formal structure for terms to ensure consistency within the ADM, and also to provide guidance for organisations that wish to implement their architecture within an architectural tool.

C. A representation of a subject of interest that provides an abstract representation of the subject.

D. A technique that, by the construction of models, enables a subject to be represented in a form that allows reasoning, insight and clarity concerning the essence of the subject matter.

Q29. Which of the following <u>best</u> defines the term metamodel?
(Select 1)

A. Data about data.

B. A candidate-physical database design.

C. A candidate-logical database design.

D. A formal structure for terms to ensure consistency within the ADM and also to provide guidance for organisations that wish to implement architectures within an architectural tool.

Q30. Which of the following <u>best</u> defines the term method?
(Select 1)

A. A formal structure for terms to ensure consistency within the ADM and also to provide guidance for organisations that wish to implement architectures within an architectural tool.

B. A defined, repeatable approach to address a particular type of problem.

C. An abstract representation of a subject of interest.

D. A technique that, by the construction of models, enables a subject to be represented in a form that allows reasoning, insight and clarity concerning the essence of the subject matter.

Q31. Which of the following <u>best</u> defines the term methodology?
(Select 1)

A. A collection of defined, repeatable steps to address a particular type of problem.

B. An abstract representation of a subject of interest.

C. A technique that, by the construction of models, enables a subject to be represented in a form that allows reasoning, insight and clarity concerning the essence of the subject matter.

D. A formal structure for terms to ensure consistency within the ADM and also to provide guidance for organisations that wish to implement architectures within an architectural tool.

Q32. Which of the following <u>best</u> defines the term model?
(Select 1)

A. Data about data.

B. A defined, repeatable approach to address a particular type of problem.

C. An abstract representation of a subject of interest.

D. A formal structure for terms to ensure consistency within the ADM and also to provide guidance for organisations that wish to implement architectures within an architectural tool.

Q33. Which of the following <u>best</u> defines the term modelling?
(Select 1)

A. A formal structure for terms to ensure consistency within the ADM and also to provide guidance for organisations that wish to implement architectures within an architectural tool.

B. A defined, repeatable approach to address a particular type of problem.

C. An abstract representation of a subject of interest.

D. A technique that, by the construction of models, enables a subject to be represented in a form that allows reasoning, insight and clarity concerning the essence of the subject matter.

Q34. Which of the following <u>best</u> defines the term objective?
(Select 1)

A. An external factor that prevents the pursuit of particular approaches to meet its goals.

B. A time-bounded milestone for an organisation used to demonstrate progress towards a goal.

C. A defined, repeatable approach to address a particular type of problem.

D. A discrete business operation or activity and how IT supports that operation.

Q35. Which of the following <u>best</u> defines the term physical?
(Select 1)

A. An abstract framework for understanding significant relationships among the entities of an environment and for the development of consistent standards or specifications supporting that environment.

B. A description of a real-world entity.

C. A candidate-solution for an Architecture Building Block.

D. An implementation-independent definition of the architecture, often grouping related, physical entities according to their purpose and structure.

Q36. Which of the following <u>best</u> defines the term reference model?
(Select 1)

A. A candidate-physical solution for an Architecture Building Block.

B. A candidate-logical solution for an Architecture Building Block.

C. An abstract framework for understanding significant relationships among the entities of an environment and for the development of consistent standards or specifications supporting that environment.

D. A formal structure for terms to ensure consistency within the ADM and also to provide guidance for organisations that wish to implement their architecture within an architectural tool.

Q37. Which of the following <u>best</u> defines the term repository?
(Select 1)

A. Part of an Enterprise Architecture related to the architectural organisation of business and covers the business strategy, governance, organisation and key business processes information, as well as the interaction between these concepts.

B. A technique that, by the construction of models, enables a subject to be represented in a form that allows reasoning, insight and clarity concerning the essence of the subject matter.

C. A system that manages all of an enterprise's data, including process models and other enterprise information.

D. An abstract framework for understanding significant relationships between the entities of an environment, and for developing of consistent standards or specifications supporting that environment.

Q38. Which of the following <u>best</u> defines the term requirement?
(Select 1)

A. The abstract representation of a related set of concerns.

B. A work package.

C. A quantitative statement of business need that must be met by a particular architectural or work package.

D. A description of a discrete business operation or activity and how IT supports that operation.

Q39. Which of the following <u>best</u> defines the term Solution Architecture?
(Select 1)

A. A formal summary description of the enterprise, providing an organising framework for operational and change activity and an executive-level, long-term view for direction setting.

B. The logical software and hardware capabilities that are required to support deployment of business, data and application services. This includes IT infrastructure, middleware, networks, communications, processing and standards.

C. A description of a discrete business operation or activity and how IT supports that operation.

D. A description of a future state of the architecture being developed for an organisation. There may be several future states developed as a roadmap to show the evolution of the architecture to a target state.

Q40. Which of the following <u>best</u> defines the term Solution Building Block?
(Select 1)

A. A constituent part of the architecture model that describes a single aspect / required capability and shapes the corresponding capability.

B. A candidate-physical solution for an Architecture Building Block.

C. A description of a discrete business operation or activity and how IT supports that operation.

D. A quantitative statement of business need that must be met by a particular architectural or work package.

Q41. **Which of the following best defines the term stakeholder?**
(Select 1)

A. An individual with interests in the outcome of the architecture.

B. An individual with concerns for the management of the final delivered solution.

C. An individual, team or organisation with interests in, or concerns relative to, the outcome of the architecture.

D. The governance board.

Q42. **Which of the following best defines the term Strategic Architecture?**
(Select 1)

A. A description of the capabilities that manage the data objects necessary to process and support the business.

B. The logical software and hardware capabilities required to support deployment of business, data and application services. This includes IT infrastructure, middleware, networks, communications, processing and standards.

C. A formal description of the enterprise, providing an organising framework for operational and change activity and an executive-level, long-term view for direction setting.

D. A description of a future state of the architecture being developed for an organisation. There may be several future states developed as a roadmap to show the evolution of the architecture.

Q43. **Which of the following best defines the term Target Architecture?**
(Select 1)

A. A description of the capabilities that manage the data objects necessary to process and support the business.

B. The logical software and hardware capabilities required to support deployment of business, data and application services. This includes IT infrastructure, middleware, networks, communications, processing and standards.

C. A description of a discrete business operation or activity and how IT supports that operation.

D. A description of a future state of the architecture being developed for an organisation. There may be several future states developed as a roadmap to show the evolution of the architecture.

Q44. **Which of the following best defines the term Technology Architecture?**
(Select 1)

A. A description of the capabilities that manage the data objects necessary to process and support the business.

B. The logical software and hardware capabilities required to support deployment of business, data and application services. This includes IT infrastructure, middleware, networks, communications, processing and standards.

C. A description of a discrete business operation or activity and how IT supports that operation.

D. A description of a future state of the architecture being developed for an organisation. There may be several future states developed as a roadmap to show the evolution of the architecture.

Q45. Which of the following <u>best</u> defines the term Transition Architecture?
(Select 1)

    A.   The logical software and hardware capabilities required to support deployment of business, data and application services. This includes IT infrastructure, middleware, networks, communications, processing and standards.

    B.   A description of a discrete business operation or activity and how IT supports that operation.

    C.   A description of a future state of the architecture being developed for an organisation. There may be several future states developed as a roadmap to show the evolution of the architecture to a target state.

    D.   A formal description of the Enterprise Architecture showing periods of transition and development for particular parts of the enterprise.

Q46. Which of the following <u>best</u> defines the term view?
(Select 1)

    A.   A visual or graphical representation of a set of concerns.

    B.   The representation of a related set of concerns.

    C.   An architecture represented by a model that manages the data objects necessary to process and support the business.

    D.   Where you are looking from; the vantage point or perspective that determines what you see.

Q47. Which of the following <u>best</u> defines the term viewpoint?
(Select 1)

    A.   A visual or graphical representation of a set of concerns.

    B.   The representation of a related set of concerns.

    C.   An individual, team or organisation with interests in, or concerns relative to, the outcome of the architecture.

    D.   Where you are looking from; the vantage point or perspective that determines what you see.

Review Your Answers

Review your answers by referring to the answers that can be found on page 181.

Further Reading and Resources

The following list provides further recommended sources of information for the areas covered by this chapter:

- TOGAF 9 Part 1 - *Introduction*, Chapter 3 (Definitions)

This chapter covers the following exam subjects:

- Architecture Views.
- Viewpoints.
- Stakeholders.

Architecture Views, Viewpoints & Stakeholders

The purpose of this chapter of the Study Guide is to understand the concepts of views and viewpoints, their role in communicating with stakeholders, and applying them to the architecture development cycle. The language used to depict a view is the viewpoint and viewpoints are customised to create a set of architecture views that cover all stakeholder concerns.

Before discussing architecture views, viewpoints and stakeholders further, it is important to first clarify the TOGAF terminology that defines them.

Architecture

An architecture is the fundamental organisation of a system's components, their relationships to each other and the principles guiding their design and development.

System

A system is a collection of components organised to accomplish a specific function or set of functions. A system can encompass individual applications, systems and sub-systems.

Stakeholders

Stakeholders can be users, developers, teams or individuals that have key roles in, or concerns about, a system. The minimum set of stakeholders for a system in which views should be developed are:

- Users
- System and software engineers
- Operators, administrators and managers
- Customers

For each stakeholder group, views may be developed that address the main categories of business, data, application and technology.

Concerns

Concerns are key interests important to stakeholders and determine the acceptability of a system. Concerns typically include functionality, performance, reliability, security and the ability to evolve. For example, a database architect would have the following concerns: authentication, data integrity, data availability, data protection, data management.

Views

A view is what you see and is a representation of a system from the perspective of a related set of concerns. A view consists of architectural models chosen by the architect to show stakeholders that their concerns are being met, and is specific to the architecture for which it is created. For example, an enterprise architect must create different views of the business, information system and technical architecture for the stakeholders who have concerns related to these aspects. These views might include business processes, physical layouts and security views of an IT system.

Viewpoints

A viewpoint is where you are looking from and defines the perspective from which a view is taken. It defines how to construct, use a view, the information it should show, the modelling techniques for expressing and analysing it. The relationship between viewpoint and view is similar to that of a template and an instance of the template. In constructing an Enterprise Architecture, an architect first selects the viewpoints (templates), then constructs a set of corresponding views (instances). Viewpoints can be generic and stored in a library for reuse: ISO/IEC 42010: 2007 encourages architects to define viewpoints that can be reused.

The architect uses views and viewpoints in the ADM cycle during phases A to D for developing architectures for each of the (business, data, application and technology) domains.

An Example View

An example view is shown in figure 7 below. The top-level relationships between geographical sites and business functions are shown. The view's modelling technique has used nested boxes where the outer boxes denote location, and the inner boxes denote business functions. The semantics of nesting are that functions are performed in those locations.

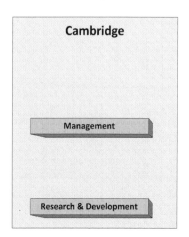

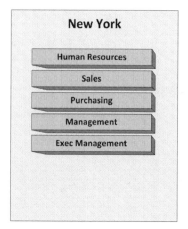
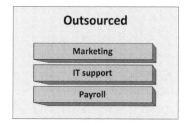

Figure 7: *Example view*

The Relationships between Views, Viewpoints, Stakeholders & Concerns

The relationships between stakeholders, concerns, views and viewpoints are summarised in figure 8 below:

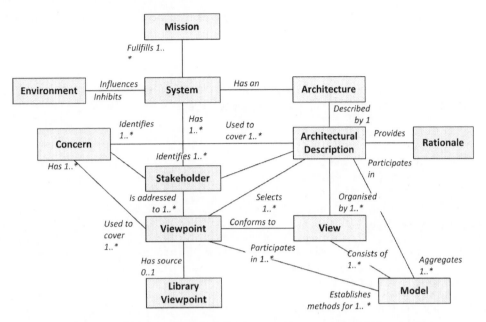

Figure 8: *The relationship between the basic architectural concepts*

The View Creation Process

The architect is responsible for developing a set of architectural views that are representations of the overall architecture shown in terms, that are meaningful to stakeholders. These views allow the architecture to be communicated to, and understood by, the stakeholders, so they can verify that the system will address their concerns.

The choice of which particular architectural views to develop is one of the key decisions that the architect has to make. The architect chooses particular views to ensure:

- The completeness of the architecture, so that it address all the concerns of its stakeholders.
- The integrity of the architecture, so that the views can be understood in relationship to each other.
- The views can be used to ensure that conflicting concerns are understood and can be reconciled.
- The views articulate what trade-offs have been made (e.g., between security and usability).

Recommended Steps

The recommended steps to create the required views for a particular architecture are:

- Select the key stakeholders.
- Analyse the stakeholders' concerns and document them.
- Refer to any existing libraries of viewpoints (TOGAF 9 includes a default set of architectural viewpoints).
- Select appropriate viewpoints (based on the stakeholders and their concerns) so that all concerns are covered by at least one viewpoint.
- Generate views of the system, using the selected viewpoints as templates.

Common Views & Viewpoints

Some of the most common views that will be developed within an architecture are:

Business Architecture View

Used to address the concerns of the users of the system, and covers views such as people, business process, business functions, usability and performance.

Data Flow View

Addresses the concerns of the database designers and administrators, covering the architecture of the storage, retrieval, processing, archiving and security of data.

Software Engineering View

Considers what software development constraints and opportunities exist in the new system and looks at how development can be carried out, both in terms of technology and software development resources.

System Engineering View

Shows how the software and hardware components will be assembled into a working system.

Communications Engineering View

Addresses the concerns of the communications engineers by showing how the networking architecture elements are to be configured and areas of interest such as bandwidth or latency constraints.

Enterprise Manageability View

Addresses the management of the system, concentrating on areas related to the security, software, data, computing hardware and communications.

Enterprise Security View

Focuses on the security aspects of the system for the protection of information within the organisation.

Exam Preparation Tasks

Review All the Key Topics

Review the most important topics from this chapter listed in table 5 below:

Description	Page
Define and explain the concept of stakeholders.	49
Define and explain the concept of concerns.	49
Define and explain the concept of views.	49
Define and explain the concept of viewpoints.	50
Describe a example of a viewpoint and view.	50
Discuss the relationship between stakeholders, concerns, views and viewpoints.	51
Describe the view creation process.	51

Table 5: *Architecture view, viewpoints and stakeholder exam syllabus checklist*

Understand the Definition of Key Terms

Define the following key terms from this chapter and check your answers:

- Stakeholders
- Concerns
- Views
- Viewpoints

Complete the Review Questions

Check your understanding of this chapter by answering the following example exam-style questions:

Q1. **Which of the following terms does TOGAF use to describe people who have concerns about a system?** **(Select 1)**

- A. Architects
- B. Consumers
- C. Sponsors
- D. Stakeholders

Q2. **Which of the following best defines the term system?**
(Select 1)

- A. A collection of components organised to accomplish a specific function or set of functions.
- B. Key interests that determine the acceptability of the system and typically include performance, reliability, security, distribution and the ability to evolve.
- C. A representation of a problem from the perspective of a related set of concerns.
- D. It defines the perspective from which a view is taken.

Q3. **Which of the following best defines the term viewpoint?**
(Select 1)

- A. A collection of components organised to accomplish a specific function or set of functions.
- B. People who have key roles in, or concerns about, the system.
- C. A representation of a system from the perspective of a related set of concerns.
- D. It defines the perspective from which a view is taken.

Q4. **Which of the following best defines the term view?**
(Select 1)

- A. A collection of components organised to accomplish a specific function or set of functions.
- B. People who have key roles in, or concerns about, a system.
- C. A representation of a system from the perspective of a related set of concerns.
- D. It defines the perspective from which a viewpoint is taken.

Q5. **Which of the following best defines the term concerns?**
(Select 1)

- A. A collection of components organised to accomplish a specific function or set of functions.
- B. People who have key roles in the system.
- C. Key interests that determine the acceptability of a system and typically include functionality, performance, reliability, security and the ability to evolve.
- D. It defines the perspective from which a viewpoint is taken.

Q6. When choosing particular architectural views to develop, the architect needs to ensure that the views are _____? (Select 1)

    A. All shown from the same single viewpoint to avoid confusing the stakeholders.

    B. Only using viewpoints for views already defined in TOGAF.

    C. Showing the completeness of the architecture so that it addresses all the concerns of its stakeholders.

    D. Showing that contracts between the architectural function and the business users are in place.

Q7. Which of the following <u>best</u> defines the term stakeholders?
(Select 1)

    A. It defines the perspective from which a view is taken.

    B. People who have key roles in, or concerns about, the system.

    C. Key interests that determine the acceptability of the system and typically include functionality, performance, reliability, security and the ability to evolve.

    D. A representation of a system from the perspective of a related set of concerns.

Review Your Answers

Review your answers by referring to the answers that can be found on page 181.

Further Reading and Resources

The following list provides further recommended sources of information for areas covered by this chapter:

- TOGAF 9 Part IV - *Architecture Content Framework*, Chapter 35 (Architectural Artefacts)

This chapter covers the following exam subjects:

- Understanding the Architecture Development Method (ADM) cycle.
- The objectives of each phase in the ADM cycle.
- Understand how to adapt and scope the ADM to the needs of the enterprise.

Introduction to the Architecture Development Method (ADM)

The purpose of this chapter of the Study Guide is to enable you to:

- Briefly describe the Architecture Development Method cycle, its phases and the objectives of each phase.
- Describe a typical set of steps, such as those for the Business Architecture Phase.
- Describe the versioning convention for deliverables used in the Architecture Development Method Phases A to D.
- Briefly describe the relationship between the ADM and other parts of TOGAF, specifically:
  - The Enterprise Continuum
  - The Architectural Repository
  - The Foundation Architecture
  - The supporting Guidelines & Techniques
- Explain the purpose of the ADM supporting Guidelines & Techniques and the difference between Guidelines and Techniques.
- Briefly describe the key points of the Architecture Development Method cycle.
- List the main reasons why you would need to adapt the Architecture Development Method.
- Explain why the Architecture Development Method process needs to be governed.
- Describe the major information areas managed by a governance repository.
- Briefly explain the reasons for scoping an architectural activity.
- List the possible dimensions for limiting the scope of the architecture activities.
- Briefly explain the need for an integration framework that sits above individual architectures.

The Architecture Development Method Cycle

The Architecture Development Method consists of a number of phases that cycle through architecture activities to ensure that a complex set of requirements is adequately addressed in the architecture. Figure 9 on page 58 shows the phases of the TOGAF Architectural Development Method process.

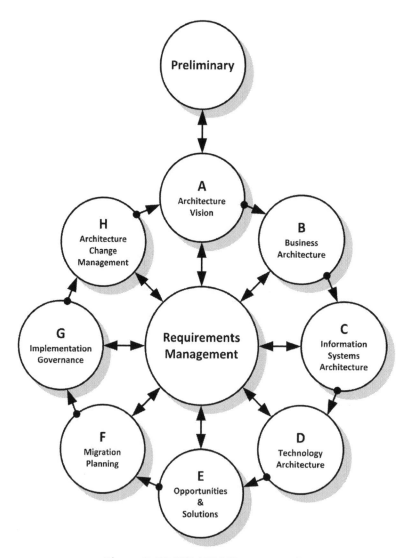

Figure 9: *TOGAF ADM Phases overview*

The ADM is applied iteratively throughout the process, between phases and within phases, with frequent validation of results against the original requirements.

Each phase should consider assets produced from previous iterations of the process and external assets, such as other frameworks or models. The ADM supports the concept of iteration at three levels:

1. **Cycling around the ADM** - the ADM is presented in a circular manner indicating that the completion of one phase of architecture work directly feeds into a subsequent phase.
2. **Iterating between ADM phases** - TOGAF describes the concept of iterating across phases. For example, the architect may return to the Business Architecture Phase on completion of the Technology Architecture Phase.
3. **Cycling around a single ADM phase** - repeated execution of the activities within a single ADM Phase may be used as a technique for elaborating architectural content in greater depth in each iteration.

Preliminary Phase

The Preliminary Phase prepares the organisation to deliver successful TOGAF architecture projects. Typical tasks in this phase are initiation activities required to meet the business directive for a new Enterprise Architecture, the definition of an organisation-specific Architecture Content Framework and the definition of Architecture Principles.

Requirements Management

Requirements are identified, stored and used in the relevant ADM Phases to address the requirements. Every stage of the TOGAF ADM is based on, and validates, business requirements (that is why they are shown at the centre of TOGAF - see Figure 9 on page 58).

Phase A - Architecture Vision

The Architecture Vision Phase sets the scope of, constraints on, and expectations for a TOGAF project by generating the Architecture Vision. The Architecture Vision defines stakeholders, validates the business context, and creates the statement of architecture work. Approvals are also obtained in this phase.

Phase B - Business Architecture, Phase C - Information System Architecture, Phase D - Technology Architecture

The Business, Information Systems, and Technology Architecture Phases of the ADM develop architectures in the following four domains:

1. Business
2. Information systems - application
3. Information systems - data
4. Technology

In each case, a Baseline Architecture and a Target Architecture are created to identify the scope of the work required to get from Baseline Architecture to the Target Architecture.

Phase E - Opportunities & Solutions

In the Opportunities and Solutions Phase, initial implementation planning is performed to identify how the building blocks identified in the previous phases will be delivered. This phase identifies implementation projects and then groups them into transition architectures that can be implemented as programmes of work.

Phase F - Migration Planning

In the Migration Planning Phase, a cost versus benefits analysis and a risk analysis with the implementation project are carried out. Migration plans are then developed in the phase.

Phase G - Implementation Governance

The Implementation Governance Phase provides the required architectural oversight for the implementation. During this phase, the Architecture Contracts will be created and issued. This phase will ensure that the implementation project conforms to the architecture (via the Implementation Governance board).

Phase H - Architecture Change Management

The Architectural Change Management Phase provides continual monitoring and change management processes to ensure that the architecture responds to the needs of the enterprise.

A Typical Set of ADM Phase Steps

Figure 10 below shows the typical steps for the Business Architecture Phase of the TOGAF ADM:

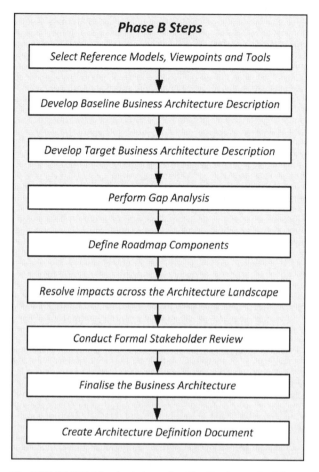

Figure 10: *TOGAF ADM typical steps for the Business Architecture phase*

The Versioning Convention for Deliverables Used in Phases A to D

The versioning of output generated through the ADM Phases needs to be managed through version numbers. Figure 11 below shows the TOGAF version numbering convention used within the ADM:

Phase	Deliverable	Content	Version	Description
A: Architecture Vision	Architectural Vision	Business Architecture	0.1	Version 0.1 indicates that a high-level outline of the architecture exists.
		Data Architecture	0.1	
		Application Architecture	0.1	
		Technology Architecture	0.1	
B: Business Architecture	Architecture Definition Document	Business Architecture	1.0	Version 1.0 indicates that a formally-reviewed, detailed architecture exists.
C: Information Systems Architecture	Architecture Definition Document	Data Architecture	1.0	
		Application Architecture	1.0	
D: Technology Architecture	Architecture Definition Document	Technology Architecture	1.0	

Figure 11: *TOGAF ADM version numbering convention*

The numbering scheme provided in the TOGAF ADM for its outputs is intended as an example only and should, therefore, be adapted by the architect to meet the specific requirements of their own organisation.

The Relationships between the ADM and Other Parts of TOGAF

This section explains the relationship between the ADM and other parts of TOGAF.

ADM, the Enterprise Continuum and Architecture Repository

The Enterprise Continuum will include reference architectures, models and patterns that have been accepted for use within the enterprise, and actual architectural work previously carried out within the enterprise.

The Enterprise Continuum provides a taxonomy and approach for the categorising and classification of architectural material. The Enterprise Continuum contains both industry reference models and the organisation's own Architecture Repository material.

The ADM makes reference to which architectural assets stored in the Architecture Repository can be used by the architect at each stage. For example, the TOGAF Foundation Architecture could be used in the development of a Technology Architecture or an industry reference model for backup used in the Technology Architecture.

By executing the ADM Phases, the architect develops both a snapshot of the enterprise at particular points in time and populates the Architecture Repository with architectural assets that can be leveraged on future architectural projects.

The first execution of the ADM is usually the hardest since there are no existing enterprise architectural assets available for reuse. However, external assets from external sources such as TOGAF and other IT industry areas can be leveraged even at this stage to seed the Architecture Repository with useful artefacts.

Architectural development in an organisation is a continuous and cyclic process: over time, the architectural practice will populate the Architecture Repository with reusable building blocks making future projects easier with more assets available for reuse.

ADM and the Foundation Architecture

The business requirements of an enterprise may be used to identify the necessary definitions and content for the Foundation Architecture. The level of detail found in the Foundation Architecture will differ depending upon the business requirements to be addressed and may range from the whole enterprise down to a restricted sub-set.

The Foundation Architecture will contain such elements as policy definitions, governance definitions and reusable common models. Specific technology selections may also be included (such as those dictated by law).

ADM and the Supporting Guidelines & Techniques

The ADM Guidelines & Techniques section of TOGAF (Part III) is a set of resources that includes templates, check-lists and other detailed materials that support the application of the TOGAF ADM. The resources are contained in a separate section to avoid cluttering the main description of the ADM itself.

The Purpose of the Supporting Guidelines & Techniques

The TOGAF guidelines describe how the ADM process can be adapted to deal with a number of different scenarios, including different process styles (e.g., the use of iteration), and also applied to specific architectures (e.g., security).

The TOGAF techniques described within the main TOGAF document in Part III support specific tasks within the ADM; for example, the gap analysis technique to identify the delta between, say, a Baseline Architecture and a Target Architecture.

The Key Points of the ADM Cycle

The TOGAF ADM follows an iterative process, with new decisions taken in iteration of the process such as:

- Enterprise coverage (whole or part)
- Level of detail and granularity
- Time period
- Architecture asset reuse:
    - Previous ADM iterations
    - Other frameworks, system models, industry models and so on.

The ADM does not recommend what the scope of each iteration covers; instead, this is left for the organisation to decide.

Decisions made at each iteration should be based on the availability (and the competence) of the architectural resources available, measured against the value that would be gained by the work done.

However, the choice of scope is critical to the success of the architectural effort. The main guideline is to focus on what creates value to the enterprise by selecting the most relevant horizontal and vertical scope. This exercise can then be iterated; building on what is being created previously to add greater breadth and depth.

The Main Reasons Why You Would Need to Adapt the ADM

The TOGAF ADM is designed to be generic and deals with most system and organisation's requirements that may have very different industry types and geographies. Because ADM is generic, TOGAF encourages organisations to tailor the ADM to suit the specific needs of the organisation. An organisation should, therefore, review the ADM process and its output to identify what is appropriate for the individual enterprise before applying the ADM. The activity of tailoring the ADM will help to produce an enterprise-specific ADM.

Some of the reasons why an individual enterprise may want to tailor the ADM are:

- The enterprise is small and requires a lighter-weight version of the ADM that is more suited to the resources available and to reduced complexity.
- The ADM Phases are dependent on the maturity of the architecture discipline within the enterprise. If the business case for doing architecture is not well recognised, then creating an Architecture Vision should be the first step. A detailed business architecture can then be developed to define the business case for the remaining architecture work. If these steps are missed out, the active participation of key stakeholders may not be secured.
- The enterprise may wish to use the ADM, in conjunction with another framework, (for example one related to defence, e-business or manufacturing) and wants to tailor the ADM so the two frameworks complement each other to reduce any overlap or duplication.

- The order of the phases may be changed to enable fast response to market changes. For example when wishing to quickly deploy a common-of-the-shelf based packaged solution, the organisation may decide to change the business processes to fit the product rather than the product being changed to fit the current business processes. In this instance, the Information Systems Architecture may well be done before the Business Architecture is completed.
- The ADM can be used to complement or support other standard programme management processes. The enterprise may, therefore, want to tailor the ADM to ensure that it integrates with other corporate processes used for corporate governance.
- The TOGAF ADM may be being used by several organisations working together on the same project (e.g., a prime contractor and several sub-contractors) with a need to tailor the ADM to achieve a suitable compromise between the existing working practices of the organisations and the enterprise's requirements.
- If the enterprise is very large or is a collection of enterprises collaborating on a project, the architecture method will need to be adapted to cope with a more federated approach.
- To adapt to deal with different use scenarios, or different process styles (e.g., the use of iteration) and to handle specific specialist architectures such as e-business or defence.

Why the ADM Process Needs to be Governed

The Architecture Development Method is a process that needs to be managed and governed to ensure that all architectural considerations are made, and all required deliverables are produced during each phase.

The management of all architectural artefacts, governance and related processes should be supported by one or more repositories supporting version control of objects, providing process control and status.

The Information Managed by a Governance Repository

The major information areas managed by a governance repository are:

- **Reference data** - used for guidance and instruction during project implementation and contains the Enterprise Continuum as well as external data (e.g., COBIT, ITIL, CMMI). The reference data should include a description of the governance procedures.
- **Process status** - a formal record of the state of any governance processes, such as outstanding compliance requests, dispensation requests, and results of compliance assessment investigations.
- **Audit information** - a formal record of all completed governance process actions used to support:
  - Key decisions (what, why) and responsible personnel (who) for any architecture project that has been sanctioned by the governance process.
  - A reference for future architectural and supporting process developments, guidance and precedence.

Reasons for Restricting the Scope of an Architecture Activity

The architecture activity may be constrained in scope for any of the following reasons:

- The availability of resources (people, finance and time)
- To address specific stakeholder concerns
- The authority of the architecture team within the organisation

Dimensions for Limiting the Scope

The scope of the architectural work is usually defined by what is feasible with the resources available at the time. The usual dimensions for limiting scope are:

Enterprise Scope or Focus (Horizontal Scope)

Defining if the scope of the architectural effort should cover the whole enterprise (which can be very large) or focus on specific areas of the enterprise.

Architecture Domains

A complete Enterprise Architecture description should contain all four architecture domains (Business, Data, Application, Technology). However, resource and/or time constraints may mean that only selected architecture domains will be covered.

Level of Detail (Vertical Scope)

The level of detail or granularity that the architectural effort goes to, as well as the boundary between where architecture effort and other activities such as system design, can be defined to constrain the scope of the architectural effort.

Time Period

A specific time period can be used to constrain what will be articulated in the Architecture Vision or any other architectural work.

The Enterprise Framework

The different architecture domains covered by the phases of the ADM needed to be integrated using an 'Enterprise Framework' such as the TOGAF Architecture Content Framework. This uses a Meta-Architecture Framework (i.e., principles, models and standards) to allow interoperability, migration and conformance between the architectures and their supporting artefacts.

Meta-Architecture Framework

The purpose of this Meta-Architecture Framework is to:

- Derive the architectural models for the enterprise-level capabilities.
- Define the conformance standards to enable maximum reuse and integration of components.
- Help the architect to understand how components fit into the framework.

The degrees to which an architecture has the 'ability to integrate'

There are varying degrees of an architecture ability to integrate:

- At the low end, the ability to integrate means that different architecture descriptions should have a 'look-and-feel' that is sufficiently similar to enable critical relationships between the descriptions to be identified. At the high end, the ability to integrate ideally means that different descriptions should be capable of being combined into a single logical and physical representation.
- Architectures that are created to address a sub-set of issues within an enterprise will require a consistent frame of reference so that they can be considered as a group, as well as individual deliverables. The scope boundary of a single architecture (e.g., level of detail and architecture domain) is typically the same as that considered for the integration of many architectures.

Exam Preparation Tasks

Review All the Key Topics

Review the most important topics from this chapter listed in table 6 below:

Description	Page
Describe the ADM cycle, its phases and the objective of each phase.	57
Describe a typical set of steps, such as those for Phase B.	60
Describe the versioning convention for deliverables used in ADM Phases A to D.	60
Describe the relationship between the ADM and other parts of TOGAF (Enterprise Continuum, Architecture Repository, Foundation Architecture, supporting Guidelines & Techniques).	61
Explain the purpose of the supporting Guidelines & Techniques and the difference between Guidelines & Techniques.	61
Describe the key points of the ADM cycle.	62
List the main reasons why you would need to adapt the ADM to your enterprise.	62
Explain the need for the ADM process to be governed.	63
Describe the major information areas managed by a governance repository.	63
List the possible dimensions for limiting the scope of architecture activity.	63
Explain the need for an integration framework that sits above individual architectures.	64

Table 6: *Introduction to the ADM exam syllabus checklist*

Understand the Definition of Key Terms

Define the following key terms from this chapter and check your answers:

- Architecture Change Management
- Architecture Vision
- Business Architecture
- Enterprise Continuum
- Enterprise Framework
- Foundation Architecture
- Governance Repository
- Implementation Governance
- Information Systems
- Migration Planning
- Opportunities & Solutions
- Preliminary Phase
- Requirements Management
- Taxonomy
- Technology Architecture

Complete the Review Questions

Check your understanding of this chapter by answering the following example exam-style questions:

Q1. **Which of the following are ADM iteration levels?**
(Select 3)
- A. Cycling around the Architecture Repository.
- B. Cycling around the ADM.
- C. Cycling around the document categorisation model.
- D. Cycling around different ADM Phases.
- E. Cycling around a single ADM Phase.
- F. Cycling around a single building block.

Q2. **What are the four architecture domains?**
(Select 4)

   A. Business
   B. Information systems - application
   C. Information systems - security
   D. Information systems - governance
   E. Information systems - data
   F. Technology

Q3. **In which phase is the Architecture Vision defined?**
(Select 1)

   A. The Preliminary Phase
   B. The Requirements Management Phase
   C. The Opportunities & Solutions Phase
   D. Phase A
   E. Phase B
   F. Phase C

Q4. **Which of the following best defines the Phase F - Migration Planning activities?**
(Select 1)

   A. Preparing the organisation for successful TOGAF architecture projects.
   B. Performing a cost versus benefit analysis, risk analysis and developing detailed Implementation plans.
   C. Setting the scope of, constraints on, and expectations for a TOGAF project.
   D. Developing the Baseline and Target Architecture and analysing gaps.
   E. Providing architectural oversight for the implementation.

Q5. **What is the first step in Phase B?**
(Select 1)

   A. Create the architecture definition document.
   B. Define roadmap components.
   C. Develop a Baseline Business Architecture description.
   D. Finalise the Business Architecture.
   E. Select reference models, viewpoints and tools.
   F. Develop a Target Business Architecture description.

Q6. **In the Business Architecture Phase, what step comes after developing the Baseline Architecture description?**   **(Select 1)**

   A. Create the architecture definition document.
   B. Define roadmap components.
   C. Develop target Business Architecture description.
   D. Finalise the Business Architecture.
   E. Select reference models, viewpoints and tools.
   F. Develop a Target Business Architecture description.
   G. Conduct a formal stakeholder review.

Q7. In which phase would a version 1.0 formally reviewed and a detailed Technology Architecture first exist? (Select 1)

A. Phase D
B. Phase E
C. Phase F
D. None of the above.

Q8. In which phase would a version 0.1 high-level outline of the Data Architecture first exist? (Select 1)

A. Phase A
B. Phase B
C. Phase C
D. Phase F
E. None of the above.

Q9. Which two phases are the same? (Select 2)

A. Phase A
B. Business Architecture
C. Phase G
D. Migration Planning
E. Technology Architecture
F. Phase H
G. Implementation Governance

Q10. Which of the following version numbers would denote a formally-reviewed, detailed Data Architecture? (Select 1)

A. 0.1
B. 0.2
C. 1.A
D. 1.0
E. A.1

Q11. Why does TOGAF say that the first execution of the ADM is usually the hardest? (Select 1)

A. The business does not understand the role that ADM will play in developing an architecture.
B. The architects are new to TOGAF and will make mistakes.
C. There are no existing enterprise architectural assets available for reuse.
D. There will be no governance structure or process in place yet.

Q12. Which statements about the Enterprise Continuum are correct? (Select 3)

A. It will contain such elements as policy and governance definitions and reusable common models.
B. It is a set of resources such as guidelines, templates, check-lists and other detailed materials that support the application of the TOGAF ADM.
C. It provides a taxonomy and approach for the categorising and classification of architectural material.
D. It will include reference architectures, models and patterns that have been accepted for use within the enterprise, and actual architectural work previously carried out within the enterprise.
E. It contains both industry reference models and the organisation's own Architecture Repository material.

Q13. Which statements about the Foundation Architecture are correct?
(Select 2)

A. It will contain such elements as policy and governance definitions and reusable common models.

B. It provides a taxonomy and approach for the categorising and classification of architectural material.

C. It may contain specific technology selections such as those dictated by law.

D. It is a set of resources such as guidelines, templates and check-lists.

E. It is a formal description of the Enterprise Architecture showing periods of transition and development for particular parts of the enterprise.

Q14. Why is there a separate section in the TOGAF documentation for ADM Guidelines & Techniques?
(Select 1)

A. To highlight their importance.

B. So that they can be easily removed when tailoring the ADM process.

C. To avoid cluttering the main description of the ADM itself.

D. They have been depreciated in TOGAF 9 and will be removed in the next version.

Q15. The TOGAF techniques described within Part III would assist in a gap analysis to identify the delta between which two types of architecture?   (Select 2)

A. Baseline Architecture

B. Target Architecture

C. Business Architecture

D. Delta Architecture

E. Data Architecture

Q16. Why does the ADM recommend the scope that each iteration covers?
(Select 1)

A. To ensure that the required level of detail is achieved in each iteration.

B. So that the phases of the ADM are not missed out.

C. To ensure that the ADM is applied effectively and fairly.

D. It doesn't: definition of the scope is left for the organisation to decide.

Q17. Which of the following is the reason why an individual enterprise may want to tailor the ADM?
(Select 1)

A. The enterprise is small and requires a lighter-weight version of the ADM.

B. The enterprise is very large or is a collection of enterprises collaborating on a project and requires a more federated approach.

C. To adapt to deal with a different usage scenarios or different process styles.

D. To use the ADM in conjunction with another framework; for example, one related to defence, e-business or manufacturing.

E. To ensure that it integrates with other corporate processes used for corporate governance.

F. All of the above.

Q18. What are the major information areas managed by a governance repository?
(Select 3)

A. Reference data

B. Process status

C. Project status

D. Audit information

E. Requirements coverage

Q19. **What are common reasons for restricting the scope of architectural activity?**
(Select 3)

    A.   The availability of resources (people, finance and time.)

    B.   To allow a gap analysis to be performed between the Baseline Architecture and the Target Architecture.

    C.   To address specific objectives or concerns of stakeholders.

    D.   The enterprise is small and requires a lighter-weight version of the ADM and reduced complexity.

    E.   The authority of the architecture team within the organisation.

Q20. **What is the purpose of a meta-Architecture Framework?**
(Select 3)

    A.   To provide a high-level view of the Architectural Vision.

    B.   To derive the architectural models for the enterprise-level capabilities.

    C.   To define the conformance standards to enable maximum reuse and integration of components.

    D.   To help the architect to understand how components fit into the framework.

    E.   To provide a low-level view of the Architecture Vision.

    F.   To develop a snapshot of the enterprise at particular point in time.

Review Your Answers

Review your answers by referring to the answers that can be found on page 181.

Further Reading and Resources

The following list provides further recommended sources of information for the areas covered by this chapter:

- TOGAF 9 Part II - *ADM*, Chapter 5 (Introduction)

This chapter covers the following exam subjects:

- The ADM Preliminary Phase.
- The ADM Architecture Vision Phase.
- The ADM Business Architecture Phase.
- The ADM Information Systems Architecture Phase.
- The ADM Technology Architecture Phase.

ADM Preliminary Phase & Phases A, B, C & D

The purpose of this chapter of the Study Guide is to ensure that you understand each of the following ADM phases:

- The Preliminary Phase.
- Phase A - Architecture Vision.
- Phase B - Business Architecture.
- Phase C - Information Systems Architecture.
- Phase D - Technology Architecture.

Preliminary Phase

The TOGAF Preliminary Phase prepares an organisation so that it is ready to undertake successful Enterprise Architecture projects.

Objectives

The objectives of the Preliminary Phase are to:

- Identify the key stakeholders, their concerns, priorities and commitment to the endeavour.
- Understand the business environment.
- Review the context in which the Enterprise Architecture work will be carried out.
- Define the Architecture Principles that are to be applied and used for evaluation of architectural work.
- Establish the require governance, business processes and support structure needed to carry out the ADM lifecycle.
- Define the framework and methodologies that will be used to develop the Enterprise Architecture (if TOGAF is to be used, then ADM process will be adopted).
- Setup the required 'architectural practice' within the organisation so that it is staffed with the people responsible for carrying out the architectural work and that their responsibilities and authority are clear to both them and the organisation.
- Assemble the required supporting infrastructure and tools for supporting the architecture activity.
- Verify the Target Architecture to ensure that it is fit-for-purpose and updated as required.
- Identify and scope the elements of the enterprise organisations affected, and define the associated constraints and assumptions.

Inputs

The inputs to the Preliminary Phase are:

- TOGAF and other architectural frameworks.
- Business strategies and plans.
- Business principles, goals and drivers.
- Governance and legal frameworks.
- Project budgets.
- Contracts and agreements.
- IT strategy.
- Existing artefacts from the Architecture Repository.

Approach

The Preliminary Phase defines the *where, what, why, who* and *how* of the architectural activity that will be performed by:

- Defining the enterprise and its boundaries.
- Defining the framework to be used.
- Defining the underpinning Architecture Principles.
- Defining the requirements for architectural work.
- Identifying key organisational drivers.
- Evaluating the Enterprise Architecture's current maturity.
- Defining the relationships between TOGAF and other management frameworks.

Outputs

The primary outputs of the Preliminary Phase are:

- The organisational model for Enterprise Architecture.
- A tailored Architectural Framework.
- An initial Architecture Repository.
- A restatement of the business principles, goals and drivers.
- Requests for architectural work.
- A governance framework.

Defining the Enterprise

The scope of the enterprise needs to be defined so that all the stakeholders who will benefit, or be affected, by the Enterprise Architecture can be identified and managed. In the Preliminary Phase, the sponsor must ensure that the architectural activity can proceed and that all relevant stakeholders are included in the scope of the architectural work.

Identifying Key Drivers and Context

The architecture will not be developed in isolation, so it is important to understand the context surrounding the architecture. As a minimum, the following areas should be considered:

- The stakeholders.
- The budget.
- The future direction and current culture of the organisation.
- The baseline Architecture Landscape.
- The current processes used for change and operation of IT.
- The skills and capabilities of the people within the enterprise.

Once the available budget, level of detail, scope and general organisation context has been defined, the architectural framework can then be tailored to the specific needs of the organisation.

Defining the Requirements for Architectural Work

The needs of the business will define the requirements and the metrics against which the solution will be measured. It is important that the sponsor ensures the following requirements are articulated by the key stakeholders in the enterprise:

- The business requirements.
- The cultural aspirations of the organisation.
- The organisation's strategic intent and direction.
- Financial requirements forecasting.

These requirements should be documented in the request for architectural work.

Defining Architecture Principles

Defining and articulating the Architecture Principles is fundamental to the development of an Enterprise Architecture. The architectural work needs to take account of business principles as well as architecture principles. Business principles will, in part, underpin and define the architecture principles.

Defining the Framework

The TOGAF ADM is generic and is intended to be used across a diverse range or enterprises, industries and geographies. The ADM can be used with a wide variety of frameworks and enhances their operational capabilities. Frameworks that are commonly used with TOGAF are:

- **Business capability management** (business direction and planning) - determines what business capabilities are required in the future.
- **Portfolio/project management methods** - determines how a company manages and controls its change initiatives through programmes of work.
- **Operations management methods** - defines how a company runs its day-to-day operations, including IT functions.
- **Solution development methods** - formalises how business systems are developed and delivered to the business.

These frameworks have significant overlaps and, as a consequence, an enterprise architect must be aware of the impact that the architecture has on the entire enterprise.

Defining the Relationships between Management Frameworks

Figure 12 on page 74 shows the dependencies between the business planning activity and various frameworks. All of the frameworks can be used within the structure of the Enterprise Architecture to address the full range of corporate initiatives.

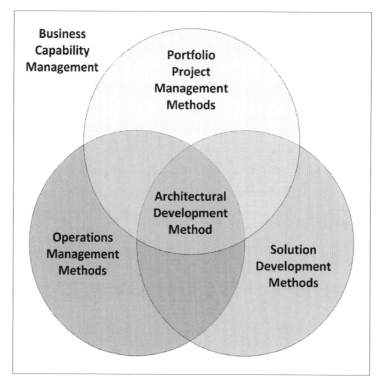

Figure 12: *Management frameworks to coordinate with TOGAF*

Figure 13 below shows the relationships between the different management frameworks and how these frameworks can complement each other and be integrated as a whole.

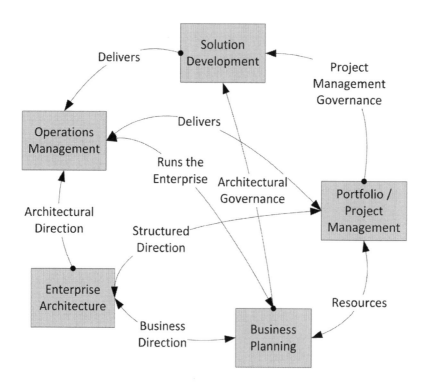

Figure 13: *Relationships between management frameworks*

Evaluating the Maturity of the Enterprise Architecture

The maturity of an Enterprise Architecture can be assessed by using Capability Maturity Models (CMMs). CMMs help the organisation to evaluate how best to develop and implement the architecture. The organisation's level of maturity can be used as a measure of the organisation's ability to change and to identify the steps required to improve its maturity level.

Principles

Principles are an initial output of the Preliminary Phase and are used throughout the ADM to provide a framework for guiding decision making within the enterprise. Principles are intended to be enduring and seldom revised. Depending on the organisation, principles may be established at any or all of the three levels defined below:

1. Enterprise Principles

Enterprise Principles provide a basis for decision making and dictate how the organisation fulfils its mission. They are a key element in a successful Architecture Governance strategy. Enterprise Principles are commonly found in governmental and commercial organisations.

2. IT Principles

IT Principles provide guidance on the use and deployment of all IT resources and assets across the enterprise to ensure that the information environment is as productive and cost-effective as possible.

3. Architecture Principles

Architecture Principles are a sub-set of IT principles that relate to architectural work. They reflect consensus and embody the spirit of the Enterprise Architecture. Architecture Principles can be further divided into:

- Principles that govern the architecture process, affecting the development, maintenance and use of the Enterprise Architecture.
- Principles that govern the implementation of the architecture.

The Standard Template for Architecture Principles

TOGAF defines a standard way of describing principles. In addition to a definition statement, each principle should have an associated rationale and implication statement, to promote understanding and to gain acceptance. The principles themselves can be used to explain and justify why specific decisions are made.

Name

Should represent the rule and be easy to remember. Specific technology platforms and ambiguous words should be avoided.

Statement

Should communicate succinctly and unambiguously the principle.

Rationale

Should highlight the business benefits of adhering to the principle, (using business terminology) and describe the relationship to other related principles. Guidance should be provided on achieving a balanced interpretation where one principle may be given precedence or carry more weight than another when making a decision.

Implications

Implications should highlight the requirements, both for the business and IT, for carrying out the principle - in terms of resources, costs and activities / tasks. The impact on the business and consequences of adopting a principle should be clearly stated. The reader should be able to easily discern the answer to: "how does this affect me?"

An Example Architectural Principle

Name - Data is a shared resource.

Statement - Users have access to the data across enterprise functions and organisations necessary to perform their duties.

Rationale - Access to accurate data is essential to the quality and efficiency of enterprise decision making. It is less costly to maintain timely, accurate, shared data in a single application than to maintain duplicate data in multiple applications.

Implications - Education is required to ensure that all organisations within the enterprise understand the relationship between the value of data, sharing of data and accessibility to data. To enable data sharing, we must develop and abide by a common set of policies, procedures and standards governing data management.

What makes a Good Architecture Principle

The criteria that distinguish a good principle are:

Comprehension

The principle should be clear, unambiguous and understandable by individuals throughout the organisation, so that violations and misunderstandings can be minimised.

Robustness

A principle should facilitate good decisions about architectures, plans, enforceable policies and standards. Each principle should be sufficiently definitive and precise to support consistent decision making in complex, potentially-controversial situations.

Completeness

The principle should cover every situation.

Consistency

Principles should not be contradictory. Strict adherence to one principle should not violate another principle. Principle statements should be carefully worded to allow consistent interpretation.

Stability

Each principle should be stable, but still able to accommodate change via an amendment process.

An Example Set of Principles

Below is an example list of principles from the US Government's Federal Enterprise Architecture Framework (FEAF):

Business Principles
- Primacy of principles.
- Maximum benefit to the enterprise.

- Information management is everyone's business.
- Business continuity.
- Common use applications.
- Service orientation.
- Compliance with law.
- IT responsibility.
- Protection of intellectual property.

Data Principles
- Data is an asset.
- Data is a shared resource.
- Data is accessible.
- Data trustee.
- Common vocabulary and data definition.
- Data security.

Application Principles
- Technology independence.
- Ease-of-use.

Technology Principles
- Requirements-based change.
- Responsive change management.
- Control technical diversity.
- Interoperability.

Phase A - Architecture Vision

The Architecture Vision Phase establishes the project and initiates an iteration of the Architecture Development Method cycle. Phase A sets the scope of, constraints on, and expectations for the iteration of architectural work.

Objectives

The objectives of the Phase A - Architectural Vision are to:

- Obtain management commitment.
- Define and organise an architecture development cycle.
- Validate Business Principles, goals, drivers and key performance indicators (KPIs).
- Identify stakeholders, their concerns and their objectives.
- Define business requirements and constraints.
- Define scope and prioritise architecture tasks.
- Articulate an Architecture Vision and value proposition to respond to the requirements and constraints by:
    - Describing the Baseline Business Architecture.
    - Developing the Target Business Architecture.
    - Analysing the gaps between the Baseline and Target Architectures.
    - Selecting architecture viewpoints to demonstrate how stakeholder concerns are addressed in the Business Architecture.

77

- Selecting tools and techniques for viewpoints.
- Create a comprehensive plan in line with the project management frameworks adopted by the enterprise.
- Understand the impact of other architecture development cycles working in parallel.
- Obtain formal approval to proceed and create the approved statement of architecture work.

Inputs

The primary inputs for Phase A - Architecture Vision consist of:

- A request for architecture work.
- The business principles, goals and drivers.
- An organisational model for Enterprise Architecture.

- A tailored Architecture Framework.
- A populated Architecture Repository.
- Reference materials external to the enterprise.

Approach

The Architecture Vision Phase will start with the receipt of a request for architecture work from the sponsoring organisation to the architecture practice. The aim of the request for architecture work is to ensure proper recognition and endorsement from corporate management and the support and commitment of line management for this iteration of the ADM cycle.

Creating the Architecture Vision is a key activity in this phase by using business scenario techniques.

Outputs

The primary outputs of the Architecture Vision Phase are:

- An approved statement of architecture work.
- Refined statements of business principles, business goals and business drivers.
- Defined Architecture Principles.
- Capability assessments.

- A tailored Architecture Framework.
- The Architecture Vision.
- A communications plan.
- Additional content populating the Architecture Repository.

Creating the Architecture Vision

The Architecture Vision will include details of how the new capability will meet the business goals and strategic objectives and address the stakeholder concerns when implemented. Therefore, the sponsor can use the Architecture Vision as a way to sell the benefits of the proposed capability to stakeholders and decision makers within the enterprise.

Key elements of the Architecture Vision, such as the enterprise mission, vision, strategy and enterprise goals may already have been documented as part of a business strategy or enterprise planning activity by the organisation. Where such documents exist, the Architecture Vision Phase will involve verifying and understanding the documented business strategy and goals. This phase may also make use of enterprise strategy and goals implicit within the current architecture.

In cases where little or no Business Architecture work has been done before, there will be a need for the architecture team to research, verify and gain buy-in to the key business objectives that the new architecture is to support.

Once the Architecture Vision has been defined and documented in the statement of architecture work, the sponsoring organisation must sign the statement of architecture work so that a consensus is reached. Without this consensus, the final architecture is unlikely to be accepted by the organisation.

In summary, the Architecture Vision provides a high-level description of the Baseline Architecture and Target Architectures, covering the business, data, application and technology domains. These high-level descriptions are then developed in subsequent ADM Phases.

Business Scenarios

A business scenario is a complete description of a business problem, both in business terms and architectural terms. A business scenario enables individual requirements to be viewed in relation to one another in the context of the overall problem.

Business scenarios are used in the Architecture Vision Phase as a technique to discover and document business requirements. Business scenarios may be used iteratively at different levels of detail in the hierarchical decomposition of the Business Architecture. An Architecture Vision can use business scenarios to demonstrate that it covers the business requirements.

Phase B - Business Architecture

In Phase B, the architect develops the Business Architecture to underpin the agreed Architecture Vision and describes the organisation's business from the perspective of:

- Showing how an organisation will meet its business goals.
- The people in the organisation.
- The business processes.
- The relationships between the business processes and the organisation's people.
- The principles governing the Business Architecture, specifically its design and evolution.

Objectives

The objectives of Phase B - Business Architecture are to:

- Describe the Baseline Business Architecture.
- Develop a Target Business Architecture.
- Perform a gap analysis between the Baseline and Target Architectures.
- Select tools and techniques for viewpoints.
- Select architecture viewpoints to demonstrate how stakeholder concerns are addressed in the Business Architecture.

Inputs

The primary inputs for Phase B - Business Architecture consist of:

- Architecture reference materials.
- A request for architectural work.
- Business principles, business goals and business drivers.
- Capability assessments.
- A communications plan.
- An organisational model for Enterprise Architecture.
- A tailored Architecture Framework.
- An approved statement of architectural work.
- Architecture Principles.
- An Enterprise Continuum.
- An Architecture Repository.
- An Architecture Vision.

Approach

An understanding of the Business Architecture is a prerequisite for the architectural work in any of the other three domains (data, application and technology) and, therefore, must be the first architectural activity undertaken. The Business Architecture can be used to demonstrate to stakeholders the business value and return on investment to be gained in supporting and participating in further architectural work. The Business Architecture will describe the product / services strategy for the organisation and describe the required functional, organisational, informational and geographic dimensions of the business.

Outputs

The primary outputs of Phase B - Business Architecture are:

- An updated statement of architecture work.
- Validated business principles, business goals and business drivers.
- Architecture Principles.
- A draft architecture definition document covering the Baseline Business Architecture, Target Business Architecture and views corresponding to the selected viewpoints addressing key stakeholder concerns.
- A draft architecture requirements specification, including the gap analysis results, technical requirements and updated business requirements.
- Business Architecture components of an Architecture Roadmap.

The Baseline Description

The baseline description can normally be obtained from existing architecture descriptions that the enterprise already has. However, the architect will need to analyse the current state from the bottom-up and to document working assumptions about the high-level architectures if no descriptions currently exist. As the work progresses the architect can begin to replace the working assumptions with fact as the details become known. This approach is in contrast to the normal approach to developing a Target Architecture which is done top-down.

Business Modelling

Business models can be developed as extensions of business scenarios developed during the Architecture Vision. Typical models will include:

- Activity models (also called 'business process models').
- Use-case models.
- Class models.

Using the Architecture Repository

During Phase B, the architecture team will also consider existing Business Architecture resources available in the Architecture Repository relevant to the current architectural work, in particular:

- Relevant Industry Architectures.
- Common Systems Architectures.
- Enterprise-specific building blocks.
- Applicable standards.

Phase C - Information Systems Architecture

In Phase C, the organisation's IT systems are documented, including the major types of information and the application systems that process them, as well as their relationships to each other and the environment.

Objectives

The objectives of Phase C are to develop:

- The Data Architecture to define the types and sources of data needed to support the business - in a way that can be understood by the stakeholders.
- The Application Architecture to define the kind of application systems needed to process the data and support the business.

Inputs

The primary inputs for Phase C - Information Systems Architecture consist of:

- Architecture reference materials.
- A request for architectural work.
- Capability assessments.
- A communications plan.
- An organisational model for Enterprise Architecture.
- A tailored Architecture Framework.

- Application principles.
- Data principles.
- A statement of architectural work.
- An Architecture Vision.
- An Architecture Repository.
- A draft architecture definition document.

Approach

Phase C will involve the development of the Data and Application Architecture. The order of the development is not prescribed by TOGAF and there are advocates for which should be done first. However, this is not discussed further as it is outside of the scope of the TOGAF Foundation Exam syllabus.

Outputs

The primary outputs of Phase C - Information Systems Architecture are:

- An updated statement of architectural work.
- The Baseline Application Architecture, Target Application Architecture, Data Architecture and Application Architecture views corresponding to the selected viewpoints addressing key stakeholder concerns.
- A draft architecture requirements specification, including gap analysis results, constraints on the Technology Architecture and updated business requirements.
- Information systems components of an Architecture Roadmap.

Key Considerations for the Data Architecture

Key considerations for the Data Architecture are:

Data Management

Data management is a key aspect of any large-scale architectural transformation undertaking by an enterprise. The effective use of data can be of significant competitive advantage to an organisation: a structured and comprehensive approach to data management is, therefore, very important.

The data management issues that must be defined, understood and addressed are:

- How and where enterprise data entities are created, stored, transported, reported, archived and disposed of.
- The data entities used by the business functions, processes and services.
- The level and complexity of data transformations required between different applications and systems.
- The requirement for software to support data integration with customers and suppliers.
- Application components that will serve as the enterprise's master data.
- Enterprise-wide standards that all application components and software packages need to adopt.

Data Migration

A critical step in deploying a new (target) application to replace the existing application is the migration of existing data. The Data Architecture should detail the data that will need to be migrated and the degree to which the data will need to be transformed for use by the target application.

The Data Architecture will also detail the data definition that will be used, initially, to support the transformation and, later, as a reference for the enterprise-wide common data definition.

Data Governance

Data Governance is required to ensure that the enterprise can make the necessary transformation:

- **Structure** - Has the enterprise the necessary organisational structure to manage the transformation?
- **Management System** - Does the enterprise have the necessary management system and data-related programmes to manage the data entities throughout the life-cycle?
- **People and Skills** - What skills and roles will the enterprise require for the transformation and does it have these skills or a plan to ensure that these skills will be obtained (e.g., through training or hiring people with the appropriate skills)?

Using the Architecture Repository

In this phase, the architecture team should consider using the relevant Data Architecture and Application Architecture resources from the organisation's Architecture Repository (or adding them if they do not yet exist).

Industry *vertical* sector Data Architecture models may be useful, such as:

- The ARTS data model for the retail industry.
- The Energistics data model for the petrochemical industry.

Industry *vertical* sector Application Architecture models such as:

- The TeleManagement Forum (TMF) - for the telecommunications industry.
- The Object Management Group (OMG) - software models relevant to specific vertical domains such as healthcare, transportation and finance.
- Application models relevant to common high-level business functions, such as e-business and supply chain management.

The Open Group has a *Reference Model* for *Integrated Information Infrastructure (III-RM)* that focuses on the application-level components and services necessary to provide a high-level integrated information infrastructure.

Phase D - Technology Architecture

In Phase D, the fundamental organisation of the IT systems is to document:

- The hardware, software and communications technology to be used.
- The relationships between the components and their relationship to the environment.
- The principles governing the design and evolution of the Technology Architecture.

Objectives

The objectives of the Technology Architecture Phase are to develop a target Technology Architecture and Architecture Roadmap that will form the basis of the subsequent implementation and Migration Planning phases.

Inputs

The primary inputs for Phase D - Technology Architecture consist of:

- Architecture reference materials.
- Product information on candidate products.
- A request for architectural work.
- Capability assessments.
- A communications plan.
- An organisational model for Enterprise Architecture.
- A tailored Architecture Framework.
- Technology principles.
- A statement of architecture work.
- An Architecture Vision.
- An Architecture Repository.
- A draft architecture definition document.
- A draft architecture requirements specification, including the business, data and Application Architecture components of an Architecture Roadmap (covering Baseline and Target Architectures for the Business, Data, Application and Technology Architectures).

Approach

During the Technology Architecture Phase, the architecture team considers what relevant Technology Architecture resources are currently available in the Architecture Repository for reuse. In particular:

- Existing IT services already deployed.
- The TOGAF Technical Reference Model (TRM).
- Generic technology models relevant to the organisation's industry sector.
- Technology models relevant to Common Systems Architectures.

Outputs

The primary outputs of Phase D - Technology Architecture are:

- An updated statement of architectural work.
- Validated technology principles or new technology principles.
- A target Technology Architecture, version 1.0 (detailed).
- A draft architecture requirements specification, including the Technology Architecture requirements.
- Technology Architecture components of an Architecture Roadmap.

Exam Preparation Tasks

Review All the Key Topics

Review the most important topics from this chapter listed in table 8 below:

Description	Page
Describe the objectives of the Preliminary Phase.	71
Explain the TOGAF phrase: 'defining the enterprise'.	72
Explain identifying key drivers and elements in the organisational context.	72
Explain defining the requirements for architectural work.	73
Explain defining Architecture Principles that will inform any architectural work.	73
Explain defining the framework to be used.	73
Explain defining the relationships between management frameworks.	73
Explain evaluating the Enterprise Architecture maturity.	75
Briefly explain the need for Architecture Principles and where they are used within TOGAF.	76
Describe the standard template for Architecture Principles.	75
Explain what makes a good Architecture Principle.	76
Describe the main objectives of the Architecture Vision Phase.	77
Explain creating the Architecture Vision in the Architecture Vision Phase.	78
Explain the use of Business Scenarios in the Architecture Vision Phase.	77
Describe the main objectives of the Business Architecture Phase.	79
Explain how the baseline description is created in the Business Architecture Phase.	80
Explain the use of business modelling in the Business Architecture Phase.	80
Explain how the Architecture Repository is used in the Business Architecture Phase.	80
Describe the main objectives of the Information Systems Architecture Phase.	81
Explain the key considerations for the Data Architecture.	81
Explain how the Architecture Repository is used in Phase C.	82
Describe the main objectives of the Technology Architecture Phase.	83
Explain how the Architecture Repository is used in the Technology Architecture Phase.	83

Table 7: *ADM overview and phases A - D exam syllabus checklist*

Understand the Definition of Key Terms

Define the following key terms from this chapter and check your answers:

- ADM
- Architecture Change Management
- Architecture Principles
- Architecture Repository
- Architecture Vision Phase
- Baseline description
- Business Architecture Phase
- Business modelling
- Business scenarios
- Capability maturity models
- Common Systems Architectures
- Data Architecture

- Data Governance
- Data Migration
- Enterprise Architecture framework
- Enterprise Architecture maturity
- Implementation Governance
- Information System Architecture Phase
- Management frameworks
- Migration Planning
- Opportunities & Solutions
- Preliminary Phase
- Technology Architecture Phase

- Technical Reference Model
- Technology Architecture Phase

Complete the Review Questions

Check your understanding of this chapter by answering the following example exam-style questions:

Q1. **Which of the following are key objectives of the TOGAF Preliminary Phase? (Select 6)**

    A. To select architecture viewpoints to demonstrate how stakeholder concerns are addressed in the Business Architecture.

    B. To understand the business environment.

    C. To ensure that the architectural endeavour has high-level management commitment and stakeholder buy-in.

    D. To Select tools and techniques for viewpoints.

    E. To obtain agreement on the scope from the relevant stakeholders and sponsors.

    F. To establish architecture principles for all architectural work.

    G. To describe the baseline Business Architecture.

    H. To establish a governance structure for the architectural work.

    I. To agree the architecture method to be adopted for the architectural work.

Q2. **TOGAF recommends that in the Preliminary Phase it is important to understand the context surrounding the architecture. Which of the following areas does TOGAF recommend be considered in this phase?** **(Select 4)**

    A. The relationships between business processes and people.

    B. The stakeholders.

    C. Implementation Governance.

    D. The budget for the Enterprise Architecture.

    E. The future direction and current culture of the organisation.

    F. The skills and capabilities of the people within the enterprise.

    G. Defining the information systems architecture.

Q3. **Which of the following key activities in the TOGAF Architecture Vision Phase allow the architect to articulate the value proposition?** **(Select 5)**

    A. Describe the Baseline Business Architecture.

    B. Develop the Target Business Architecture.

    C. Obtain agreement on scope from the relevant stakeholders and sponsors.

    D. Understand the business environment.

    E. Analyse the gaps between the Baseline and Target Architectures.

    F. Select architecture viewpoints to demonstrate how stakeholder concerns are addressed in the Business Architecture.

    G. Establish a governance structure for the architectural work.

    H. Select tools and techniques for creating viewpoints.

Q4. **How often would the Preliminary Phase be carried out by an organisation? (Select 1)**

    A. Each time architectural work is required.

    B. Each time the ADM is tailored by the organisation.

    C. Once only.

    D. Whenever the Baseline Architecture changes.

    E. Whenever the Target Architecture changes.

    F. When a new release of TOGAF is used by the organisation.

Q5. **What activities are done in the Architecture Vision Phase at the start of every architecture cycle?**
(Select 3)

- A. Describe the Baseline Business Architecture.
- B. Create the approved statement of architecture work.
- C. Validate the business context.
- D. To select tools and techniques for creating viewpoints.
- E. Creating the Architecture Vision.
- F. Selecting architecture viewpoints to demonstrate how stakeholder concerns are addressed in the Business Architecture.

Q6. **Which of the following are objectives of the Architecture Visioning Phase?**
(Select 6)

- A. Obtain management commitment and obtain formal approval to proceed.
- B. Establish an Architecture Change Management process for the new Enterprise Architecture baseline.
- C. Define and organise an architecture development cycle.
- D. Validate Business Principles, goals, drivers and Key Performance Indicators (KPIs).
- E. Develop the Application Architecture to define the kind of application systems needed to process the data and support the business.
- F. Identify stakeholders, their concerns, objectives and define business requirements and constraints.
- G. Develop the Data Architecture to define the types and sources of data needed to support the business in a way that can be understood by the stakeholders.
- H. Define, scope and prioritise architecture tasks and articulate an Architecture Vision and value proposition to respond to the requirements and constraints.
- I. Create a comprehensive plan inline with the project management frameworks adopted by the enterprise and understand the impact of other architecture development cycles working in parallel.

Q7. **Which of the following activities are parts of the Architecture Vision Phase?**
(Select 5)

- A. Consider what relevant Data Architecture and Application Architecture resources are available in the organisation's Architecture Repository.
- B. Define a series of Transition Architectures that deliver business capability increments allowing for continuous business value to be generated.
- C. Develop a Target Technology Architecture that will form the basis of the subsequent implementation and Migration Planning Phases.
- D. Define an implementation programme that will enable the delivery of the agreed Transition Architectures taking the enterprise from its current Baseline Architecture through to the final Target Architecture.
- E. Confirm the Transition Architectures defined in the Opportunities & Solutions Phase with the stakeholders.
- F. Define how the new capability will meet the business goals and strategic objectives and address the stakeholder concerns when implemented.
- G. Make use of the enterprise strategy and goals implicit within the current architecture.
- H. Ensure that the sponsoring organisation signoff the statement of architecture work so that a consensus across the whole organisation is reached.
- I. Provide a high-level description of the Baseline Architecture and Target Architectures covering the business, data, application and technology domains.

Q8. In Phase B, the architect develops the Business Architecture to underpin the agreed Architecture Vision and describes the organisation's business from which of the following perspectives? **(Select 5)**

A. The organisation's people.

B. The business processes.

C. The relationships between the business processes and the organisation's people.

D. The relationships between the business processes and the business goals.

E. The principles governing the Business Architecture, specifically its design and evolution.

F. How the ADM process will be managed via the governance process.

G. The translation from the Baseline Architecture to the Target Architecture.

H. How an organisation will meet its business goals.

Q9. Which of the following are objectives of the Business Architecture Phase? **(Select 5)**

A. Develop the target Technology Architecture.

B. Describe the Baseline Business Architecture.

C. Develop a Target Business Architecture.

D. Confirm the Transition Architectures defined in the Opportunities & Solutions Phase with the stakeholders.

E. Analyse the gaps between the Baseline and Target Architectures.

F. Select architecture viewpoints to demonstrate how stakeholder concerns are addressed in the Business Architecture.

G. Prioritise all work packages, projects and building blocks by assigning business values to each and conducting a cost / benefit analysis.

H. Select tools and techniques for viewpoints.

Q10. Which of the following statements are true about the Business Architecture Phase? **(Select 3)**

A. An understanding of the Business Architecture is a prerequisite for starting architectural work in any of the other three domains (data, application and technology).

B. In this Phase, the architecture team considers what relevant Technology Architecture resources are currently available in the Architecture Repository for reuse.

C. The Business Architecture can be used to demonstrate to stakeholders the business value and 'Return on Investment' to be gained in supporting and participating in further architectural work.

D. This Phase provides a high-level description of the Baseline Architecture and Target Architectures, covering the business, data, application and technology domains.

E. During this Phase, the architecture team will also consider what existing Business Architecture resources are available from the Architecture Repository relevant to the architectural work.

F. The goal of the Business Architecture Phase is to ensure that the solution architectural will deliver the target business value.

Q11. Which of the following are the two steps in Phase C which may be developed either sequentially or concurrently?   (Select 2)

A.   Data Architecture

B.   Baseline Architecture

C.   Transition Architectures

D.   High-level Architecture

E.   Application Architecture

F.   Component Architecture

G.   Business Architecture

H.   Target Architecture

Q12. Which of the following are the key considerations for the Data Architecture?
(Select 3)

A.   Data management

B.   Information management

C.   Data migration

D.   Security and access control

E.   Data Governance

F.   Data recovery

G.   Data integrity

H.   Data backup

I.   Data volumes

Q13. In which three areas is Data Governance required to ensure that the enterprise can make the necessary transformation?   (Select 3)

A.   Organisational structure

B.   Stakeholder management

C.   Management systems

D.   Migration vision

E.   People & skills

F.   Data standards

Q14. What is the objective of the Technology Architecture Phase?
(Select 1)

A.   Finalise the Architecture Vision and architecture definition documents.

B.   Confirm the Transition Architectures defined in the Opportunities & Solutions Phase with the stakeholders.

C.   Develop the Data Architecture to define the types and sources of data needed to support the business in a way that can be understood by the stakeholders.

D.   Develop a target Technology Architecture that will form the basis of the subsequent implementation and Migration Planning Phases.

E.   Develop the Application Architecture to define the kind of application systems needed to process the data and support the business.

Q15. During the Technology Architecture Phase, which of the following resources will the architecture team consider for reuse from the Architecture Repository? (Select 4)

A. Existing IT services already deployed in the enterprise.

B. The TOGAF Technical Reference Model (TRM).

C. Existing migration plans.

D. Generic technology models relevant to the organisation's industry sector.

E. Activity models (also called business process models).

F. The statement of architectural work.

G. Technology models relevant to Common Systems Architectures.

Q16. Which part of the TOGAF template for defining Architecture Principles should highlight the business benefits of adhering to the principle? (Select 1)

A. Implications

B. Name

C. Rationale

D. Statement

E. Benefits

F. Justifications

Review Your Answers

Review your answers by referring to the answers that can be found on page 182.

Further Reading and Resources

The following list provides further recommended sources of information for the areas covered by this chapter:

- TOGAF 9 Part II - *ADM Phases* - Preliminary to Phase H and Requirements Management (Chapters 6 to 17)
- Website: http://www.volere.co.uk/template.htm

This chapter covers the following exam subjects:

- The ADM Opportunities & Solutions Phase
- The ADM Migration Planning Phase
- The Implementation Governance Phase
- The Architecture Change Management Phase
- Requirements Management

CHAPTER 8

ADM Phases E to H & Requirements Management

The purpose of this chapter of the Study Guide is to ensure that you understand the following ADM Phases:

- Phase E - Opportunities & Solutions.
- Phase F - Migration Planning.
- Phase G - Implementation Governance.
- Phase H - Architecture Change Management.
- Requirements Management.

Phase E - Opportunities & Solutions

The Opportunities & Solutions Phase is concerned with implementation and describes the process of defining projects that will deliver the target architecture generated in the ADM Phases B, C and D.

Key activities in this phase are:

- Starting implementation planning.
- Identifying the major implementation projects.
- Grouping projects into transition architectures that will deliver new business capability.
- Identifying dependencies.
- Assessing priorities.
- Deciding on approaches to be taken with regard to:
    - Make, buy or reuse decisions.
    - Outsourcing.
    - Use of commercial-off-the-shelf (COTS) products.
    - Use of Open Source products.

Objectives

The objectives of the Opportunities & Solutions Phase E are to:

- Review the objectives and capabilities of the target business.
- Consolidate the gaps from the ADM Phases B, C & D, assemble groups of building blocks to address these capabilities, and define the first complete version of the Architecture Roadmap.
- Confirm the enterprise's capability for undergoing the required change.
- Define a series of Transition Architectures that deliver business increments of capability allowing for continuous business value to be generated.

- Ensure that the organisation has a consensus on the implementation and migration strategies.

Inputs

The primary inputs for the Opportunities & Solutions Phase are:

- Architecture reference materials.
- Product information.
- A request for architecture work.
- A capability assessment.
- A communications plan.
- Planning methodologies.
- An organisational model for Enterprise Architecture.
- Governance models and frameworks.
- A tailored Architecture Framework.
- A statement of architecture work.

Approach

The Opportunities & Solutions Phase concentrates on how to deliver the architecture and views the architecture from both a corporate business and a technical perspective. The aim is to rationalise the IT activities and group them into logical project work packages. This requires a collaborative effort between the enterprise stakeholders and IT to assess the organisation's business transformation readiness, to identify opportunities, solutions and identify implementation constraints.

The transition from development to delivery requires this phase focus on business value, flexibility, co-ordination and compromise.

Outputs

The outputs for the Opportunities & Solutions Phase are:

- Refined and updated versions of the Architecture Vision, Business Architecture, Information Systems Architecture and Technology Architecture Phase deliverables.
- A consolidated and validated Architecture Roadmap that details individual work packages against a timeline that will deliver the Target Architecture.
- Capability assessments.
- A Transition Architecture, version 1.0.
- An implementation and migration plan, version 0.1, including a high-level implementation and migration strategy.

Phase F - Migration Planning

The Migration Planning Phase addresses how to move from the current Baseline Architecture to the new target architectures.

Objectives

The objectives of the Migration Planning Phase are to:

- Finalise the Architecture Vision, architecture definition and Architecture Roadmap documents.
- Confirm the transition architectures defined in the Opportunities & Solutions Phase with the stakeholders.
- Prioritise all work packages, projects and building blocks by assigning business value to each and conducting a cost / benefit analysis so that the assigned priorities are understood by the stakeholders.
- Create and refine the detailed implementation and migration plan.
- Ensure that the implementation and migration plans are coordinated with any other management frameworks used within the enterprise.

- Provide the necessary resources to enable the realisation of the Transition Architectures.
- Monitor the detailed implementation and migration plans as the architectural work progresses.

Inputs

The primary inputs for the Migration Planning Phase consist of:

- Architecture reference materials.
- Product information.
- A request for architecture work.
- A capability assessment.
- A communications plan.
- An organisational model for Enterprise Architecture.
- Governance models and frameworks.
- A tailored Architecture Framework.
- A statement of architecture work.
- An Architecture Vision.
- An Architecture Repository.
- A draft architecture definition document.
- A draft architecture requirements specification.
- Change requests for existing business programs and projects.
- A consolidated and validated Architecture Roadmap.
- A Transition Architecture, version 1.0.
- An implementation and migration plan, version 0.1, including a high-level implementation and migration strategy.

Approach

The focus of the Migration Planning Phase is to create an implementation and migration plan with the programme and project managers. This phase will involve assessing the costs versus benefits of the various migration projects, and the dependencies they may have, to arrive at a prioritised list of projects for the detailed implementation and migration plan. This project-level detail will supplement the architectures and allow tasks to be allocated to specific resources.

Outputs

The outputs for Phase F - Migration Planning are:

- An implementation and migration plan, version 1.0.
- A finalised architecture definition document.
- A finalised architecture requirements specification.
- A finalised Architecture Roadmap.
- A finalised Transition Architecture.
- A set of reusable Architecture Building Blocks.
- Requests for architectural work.
- Architecture Contracts for implementation projects.
- An Implementation Governance model.
- Change requests arising from lessons learned.

Phase G - Implementation Governance

The Implementation Governance Phase monitors the implementation projects to ensure that they follow the defined architecture and ensures that a signed Architecture Contract is produced.

Objectives

The objectives of the Implementation Governance Phase are to:

- Define the architecture constraints for the implementation projects.

- Ensure that each project conforms to the Target Architecture and the Baseline Architecture remains fit for purpose.
- Govern and manage the Architecture Contracts, assess the performance of the architecture, and to make recommendations for change, as required.
- Ensure the solution is deployed successfully as part of a planned programme of work.
- Put in place support operations that will underpin the deployed solution throughout its lifetime.
- Monitor implementation work for conformance with the architecture, provide architectural oversight for the implementation, and, to operate the governance process.

Inputs

The primary inputs for the Implementation Governance Phase consist of:

- Architecture reference materials.
- A request for architectural work.
- A capability assessment.
- An organisational model for Enterprise Architecture.
- A tailored Architecture Framework.
- A statement of architectural work.
- An Architecture Vision.
- An Architecture Repository.
- An architecture definition document.
- An architecture requirements specification.
- An Architecture Roadmap.
- A capability assessment.
- The Transition Architecture.
- An Implementation Governance model.
- Architecture Contracts.
- An implementation and migration plan.

Approach

The Implementation Governance Phase runs in parallel with the development phase of the architecture, bringing together all the implementation projects, and ensures that they comply with the defined architectures.

The approach taken is to:

- Define an implementation program with the project managers that will enable the delivery of the agreed transition architectures taking the enterprise from its current baseline architecture through to the final target architecture.
- Ensure that the phased deployment schedule reflects the business priorities embodied in the Architecture Roadmap.
- Ensure compliance with the organisation's standard for corporate, IT and Architecture Governance.
- Use the organisation's existing programme management approach.
- Ensure the effective life of the deployed solution by defining the operations framework needed to support it.

Outputs

The outputs for the Implementation Governance Phase are:

- Signed Architecture Contracts.
- Compliance assessments.
- Change requests.
- Architecture-compliant solutions.
- A populated Architecture Repository.
- Architecture compliance recommendations and dispensations.
- Recommendations on service delivery requirements.
- Recommendations on performance metrics.
- Service level agreements (SLAs).

- An Architecture Vision, updated post-implementation.
- An architecture definition document, updated post-implementation.
- The Transition Architecture, updated post-implementation.
- Business and IT operating models for the implemented solution.

Phase H - Architecture Change Management

The Architecture Change Management Phase ensures that changes to the architecture are managed in a controlled manner. The key activities include:

- Providing continual monitoring of architectural projects.
- Providing a change management process and ensuring that any changes to the architecture are properly controlled and managed.
- Providing a flexible approach to deal with changes in the technology or business environment.
- Monitoring both the business and capacity management.

Objectives

The objectives of the Architecture Change Management Phase are to:

- Operate the governance framework.
- Establish an Architecture Change Management process.
- Maximise the business value to be obtained from the architecture and on-going operations.
- Ensure that the Baseline Architecture is updated and continues to be fit for purpose.
- Assess changes to the framework and principles set up in previous phases.
- Assess the performance of the architecture and make recommendations for any changes required.

Inputs

The primary inputs for the Architecture Change Management Phase consists of:

- Architecture reference materials.
- A request for architecture work.
- An organisational model for Enterprise Architecture.
- A tailored Architecture Framework.
- A statement of architectural work.
- An Architecture Vision.
- An Architecture Repository.
- An architecture definition document.
- An architecture requirements specification.
- An Architecture Roadmap.
- A change request for technology, business and arising from lessons learned.
- The Transition Architecture.
- An Implementation Governance model.
- Signed Architecture Contracts.
- Compliance assessments.
- An implementation and migration plan.

Approach

The goal of the Architecture Change Management Phase is to ensure that the architecture will deliver the target business value. The Architecture Change Management process will determine:

- The circumstances under which the Enterprise Architecture will be permitted to change after deployment.
- The process by which any changes to the Enterprise Architecture will be allowed.
- The circumstances under which the architecture development cycle will be initiated to develop a new architecture.

Outputs

The outputs for the Architecture Change Management Phase are:

- Architecture updates (for maintenance changes).
- Changes to the Architecture Framework and principles (for maintenance changes).
- A new request for architectural work.
- A statement of architectural work.
- An Architecture Contract.
- Compliance assessments.

Drivers for Change

The three ways to change the existing architecture through:

1. A strategic, top-down, directed change to enhance an existing capability or to create a new capability.
2. A bottom-up change to correct or enhance capability (operations and maintenance) for infrastructure.
3. Feedback and experience gained from the previously delivered project increments.

Enterprise Architecture Change Management Process

The Enterprise Architecture Change Management process must define the techniques and methodologies used to manage changes. TOGAF recommends classifying the required architectural changes into one of three categories:

1. **Simplification change** - to reduce investment. This is usually handled via change management techniques.
2. **Incremental change** - to derive additional value from an existing investment. This may be handled either via change management techniques or it may require partial re-architecting.
3. **Re-architecting change** - to increase investment in order to create new value for exploitation. This will require the whole architecture to go through the Architecture Development Method cycle.

Heuristics for Classifying Change

A good set of heuristics for classifying changes are:

- If the change impacts only one stakeholder, it is more likely to be a candidate for change management.
- If the change can be allowed under a dispensation, then it is more likely to be a candidate for change management.
- If the change impacts two or more stakeholders, the impact is significant for the business strategy and is likely to require an architecture redesign.
- If the change is related to new technology, or if a new standard emerges, there may be a need to refresh the Technology Architecture, but not the whole Enterprise Architecture - so an incremental change to just the Technology Architecture may be the most appropriate.
- If the change is at an infrastructure level and does not affect the architecture above the physical layer, this change can be handled via change management.

Refreshment cycles tend to be needed when:

- The business strategy has changed and the Foundation Architecture needs to be realigned.
- Standards used in the product architecture have changed which have significant end-user impact; for example, regulatory changes.
- There has been substantial change to components of the architecture.
- The guidelines for use in deployment of the architecture have changed significantly.

When a new refreshment cycle is required, a new request for architectural work will need to be issued.

Requirements Management

The Requirements Management process is at the very centre of the ADM. It addresses the identification of requirements for the enterprise, stores them, and allows them to be used in all ADM Phases.

Objectives

The objectives of Requirements Management are to:

- Identify requirements for the enterprise.
- Manage architecture requirements throughout all phases of the ADM cycle.
- Provide a process for the storage, retrieval, modification and disposal of requirements for use by ADM Phases.

Inputs

The primary inputs for Requirements Management consist of:

- A populated Architecture Repository.
- An organisational model for Enterprise Architecture.
- A tailored Architecture Framework.
- A statement of architectural work.
- An Architecture Vision.
- Architectural requirements, populating an architecture requirements specification.
- A requirements impact assessment.

Approach

The ability to deal with changes in requirements is crucial and the ADM is continuously driven by the Requirements Management process. Architecture deals with uncertainty and change, therefore tools for bridging the divide between the aspirations of the stakeholders and what can be delivered as a practical solution are required. TOGAF does not mandate or recommend any specific process or tool for Requirements Management but simply states that an effective Requirements Management process should be used. TOGAF does, however, suggest a number of resources in this area.

Business Scenarios

Business scenarios are a technique to discover and document business requirements and to describe an Architecture Vision that responds to those requirements.

Volere Requirements Specification Template

The Volere requirements specification template is a requirements template, which is freely available and may be modified or copied (for internal use, provided the copyright is appropriately acknowledged). An extract of the template can be found on the Volere website: http://www.volere.co.uk/template.htm

Outputs

The outputs of Requirements Management are:

- A requirements impact assessment.
- An updated architecture requirements specification.

Exam Preparation Tasks

Review All the Key Topics

Review the most important topics from this chapter listed in table 8:

Description	Page
Describe the main objectives of the Opportunities & Solutions Phase.	91
Explain the approach in the Opportunities & Solutions Phase.	92
Describe the main objectives of the Migration Planning Phase.	92
Explain the approach in the Migration Planning Phase.	93
Describe the main objectives of the Implementation Governance Phase.	93
Explain the approach in the Implementation Governance Phase.	93
Describe the main objectives of the Architecture Change Management Phase.	95
Explain the approach in the Architectural Change Management Phase.	95
Explain drivers for change in the Architectural Change Management Phase.	96
Explain the Enterprise Architecture Change Management process.	96
Explain the guidelines for maintenance versus architecture redesign.	96
Briefly explain how Requirements Management fits into the ADM cycle.	97
Describe the objectives of the Requirements Management process.	97
Describe the approach to Requirements Management.	97

Table 8: *ADM Phases E to H and Requirements Management exam syllabus checklist*

Understand the Definition of Key Terms

Define the following key terms from this chapter and check your answers:

- Transition Architectures
- Migration Planning
- Architecture definition
- Implementation Governance
- Architecture Change Management

- Requirements Management
- Business scenarios
- Common-off-the-Shelf (COTS)
- Open Source

Complete the Review Questions

Check your understanding of this chapter by answering the following example exam-style questions:

Q1. **In which ADM Phase is an Architecture Contract developed to cover the overall implementation and deployment process?**   (Select 1)

A. Phase E

B. Phase F

C. Phase G

D. Phase A

Q2. Which of the following are key activities in the Opportunities & Solutions Phase?
(Select 3)

A. Finalise the Architecture Vision and architecture definition documents.

B. Implementation planning and identifying the major implementation projects.

C. Grouping projects into Transition Architectures that will deliver new business capability.

D. Identify dependencies, assess priorities and decide on approaches to be taken with regard to outsourcing, use of COTS and Open Source products.

E. Confirm the Transition Architectures defined in the Opportunities & Solutions Phase with the stakeholders.

F. Obtain sign-off for the statement of architecture work.

Q3. The Opportunities & Solutions Phase concentrates on how to deliver the architecture. What are the key areas that this phase needs to focus on?   (Select 4)

A. Integrity

B. Governance

C. Architecture Vision

D. Business value

E. Flexibility

F. Co-ordination

G. Compromise

Q4. What are the major objectives of the Migration Planning Phase?
(Select 4)

A. To finalise the Architecture Vision, architecture definition documents and confirm the Transition Architectures defined in the Opportunities & Solutions Phase with the stakeholders.

B. Prioritise all work packages, projects and building blocks by assigning business value to each and conducting a cost versus benefit analysis.

C. Define a series of transition architectures that deliver business capability increments allowing for continuous business value to be generated. Ensure that the organisation has a consensus on the implementation and migration strategies.

D. Consolidate the gaps from the ADM Phases B, C & D and then assemble groups of building blocks to address these capabilities. Confirm the enterprise's capability for undergoing the required change.

E. Create and refine the detailed implementation and migration plan. Ensure that the implementation and migration plan is co-ordinated with the management frameworks used within the enterprise.

F. Provide the necessary resources to enable the realisation of the Transition Architectures. Monitor the detailed implementation and migration plan as the architectural work progresses.

Q5. In which ADM Phase should lessons learned be documented to enable continuous process improvement?   (Select 1)

A. Phase B

B. Phase D

C. Phase F

D. Phase G

E. Phase H

F. All of the ADM Phases.

G. None, this is not part of TOGAF.

Q6. Which of the following are key activities in the Implementation Governance Phase?
(Select 3)

A. Ensuring that the Baseline Architecture remains fit-for-purpose through the implementation stage, assessing the performance of the architecture and making recommendations for change.

B. Consolidating the gaps from the ADM Phases D, E & F and defining projects to address these capabilities. Then, confirm the enterprise's capability for undergoing the required change.

C. Defining the architecture constraints for the implementation projects providing architectural oversight for the implementation, and operating the governance process.

D. Governing and managing the Architecture Contracts and monitoring implementation work for conformance with the architecture.

E. Creating and refining the detailed implementation and migration plan. Ensuring that the implementation and migration plan is coordinated with the various management frameworks in use within the enterprise.

F. Prioritising all work packages, projects and building blocks by assigning business value to each and conducting a cost / benefit analysis.

Q7. Which of the following are key activities in the Architectural Change Management Phase?
(Select 4)

A. Prioritising all work packages, projects and building blocks by assigning business value to each and conducting a cost / benefit analysis.

B. Providing continual monitoring of architectural projects.

C. Providing a change management process and ensuring that any changes to the architecture are properly controlled and managed.

D. Providing a flexible approach to deal with changes in the technology or business environment.

E. Creating and refining the detailed implementation and migration plan. Ensuring that the implementation and migration plan is co-ordinated with the various management frameworks in use within the enterprise.

F. Monitoring the business and capacity management.

Q8. TOGAF recommends classifying the required architectural changes into one of three categories; which of the following are TOGAF categories? (Select 3)

A. A simplification change, often driven by a requirement to reduce investment.

B. An incremental change, driven by a requirement to derive additional value from an existing investment

C. A translation change, driven by the need to provide a step-wise refinement and deployment solution.

D. A requirements change, driven by a change to the business requirements.

E. A re-architecting change, driven by a requirement to increase investment in order to create new value for exploitation.

F. An operation change, driven by a change to the existing infrastructure into which the new architecture must be tailored to be accommodated.

Q9. Which of the following types of changes may require an architectural redesign?
(Select 2)

A. An infrastructure level change that does not affect the architecture above the physical layer.

B. A change allowed under a dispensation.

C. A change that impacts on two or more stakeholders.

D. A change that affects only one stakeholder.

E. A change related to a new emerging technology.

Q10. **Which of the following changes would probably require an architectural refreshment cycle? (Select 3)**

    A. The business strategy has changed and the Foundation Architecture needs to be realigned.

    B. The standards used in the product architecture have changed, which have significant end-user impact; for example, regulatory changes.

    C. There has been minimal change to components of the architecture.

    D. The guidelines for use in deployment of the architecture have changed significantly.

    E. A change that affects only one stakeholder.

Q11. **Which of the following are the <u>best</u> objectives of Requirements Management? (Select 3)**

    A. Identify requirements for the enterprise.

    B. Provide a process for the storage of requirements for use by ADM Phases.

    C. Manage architecture requirements throughout Phases A to D of the ADM cycle.

    D. Provide a process for the storage, retrieval, modification and disposal of requirements for use by ADM Phases.

    E. Manage architectural requirements throughout all ADM phases.

Review Your Answers

Review your answers by referring to the answers that can be found on page 182.

Further Reading and Resources

The following list provides further recommended sources of information for the areas covered by this chapter:

- TOGAF 9 Part II - *ADM Phases* - Preliminary to Phase H and Requirements Management (Chapters 6 to 17)
- Website: http://www.volere.co.uk/template.htm

This chapter covers the following subject:

- ADM Deliverables.

CHAPTER 9

ADM Deliverables

The purpose of this chapter of the Study Guide is to ensure that you understand the key deliverables of the ADM cycle and the TOGAF terminology used to describe them.

The ADM Deliverables

You need to be able to describe and explain the following:

- The role of architectural deliverables across the ADM cycle.
- The purpose of the following deliverables:

  - Architecture Building Blocks
  - Architecture Contracts
  - An architecture definition document
  - Architecture Principles
  - An Architecture Repository
  - Architecture requirements specification
  - An Architecture Roadmap
  - An Architecture Vision
  - Business drivers
  - Business goals
  - Business principles
  - Capability assessment
  - Change requests
  - A communications plan
  - Compliance assessment
  - An Implementation and Migration Plan
  - An Implementation Governance Model
  - An organisational model for Enterprise Architecture
  - A request for architectural work
  - A requirements impact assessment
  - Solution Building Blocks
  - A statement of architectural work
  - A tailored Architecture Framework
  - Transition Architecture

The Role of Architecture Deliverables

TOGAF defines a set of deliverables produced and used throughout the ADM cycle. The TOGAF deliverables are a typical set of architecture deliverables that can be used as a starting point for any organisation. These baseline deliverables can then be tailored to the organisation's specific needs.

Architecture deliverables are usually contractual and formal work products on a project; they will, therefore, be constrained or affected by the overall project's processes, such as CMMI, PRINCE2 and PMBOK.

Architecture Deliverables

This section describes the purpose of deliverables produced and consumed throughout the TOGAF ADM cycle.

Architecture Building Blocks

An Architecture Building Block is a constituent part of the architecture model that describes a single aspect / required capability. It will shape the corresponding Solution Building Block(s) that will implement the capability.

Architecture Contracts

Architecture Contracts occur at various stages of the ADM and define joint agreements between development partners and sponsors on the deliverables, as well as the quality and fitness for purpose of architecture. Architecture Contracts are normally produced in the Governance Phase.

Architecture Definition Document

The architecture definition document contains the core architectural deliverables created during a project. It spans the business, data, application and technology domains and examines all relevant states of the architecture (baseline, interim state(s) and target).

The architecture definition document is created in Phases A and B when it is populated with the Architecture Vision and Business Architecture-related material. It is subsequently updated with Information Systems Architecture material (data / application) in Phase C and then finally completed with Technology Architecture material in Phase D.

The architecture definition document is a companion to the architecture requirements specification, providing a qualitative and quantitative view of the solution, stating measurable criteria that must be met during the implementation of the architecture.

Architecture Principles

Architecture Principles define the underlying general rules and guidelines for the use and deployment of all IT resources and assets across the enterprise. Each Architecture Principle should be clearly related to the business objectives and key architecture drivers that they are to support.

Principles are general rules and guidelines, intended to be enduring and seldom amended. Principles inform and support the way in which an organisation sets about fulfilling its mission. Principles are, essentially, a set of ideas that collectively define and guide the organisation - from values through to actions and results.

Architecture Repository

The Architecture Repository is a storage area for all architecture-related projects within the enterprise. It allows projects to manage their deliverables, locate reusable assets, and to publish outputs to stakeholders.

Architecture Requirements Specification

The architecture requirements specification provides a set of quantitative statements that outline what an implementation project must do in order to comply with the architecture. Each requirement in the specification describes a condition or capability to which a system must conform - either derived directly from user needs; or stated in a contract, standard, specification, or other formally imposed document. An architecture requirements specification will, typically, form a major component of an implementation contract and is a companion to the architecture definition document.

Architecture Roadmap

The Architecture Roadmap provides an ordered sequence of increments of change to progress from a Baseline Architecture to the Target Architecture. The Architecture Roadmap forms a key component of Transition Architectures (developed in Phases E and F) and is incrementally developed throughout phases B, C, D, E and F within the ADM. The Architecture Roadmap is aligned to the business roadmap that shows the programme activities and planned delivery projects.

Architecture Vision

The Architecture Vision is created in Phase A and defines the desired outcome for the architecture by providing a high-level, aspirational view. The Architecture Vision supports stakeholder communication by providing an executive summary version of the full architecture definition.

Architects use the Architecture Vision to focus on critical areas in order to validate the architecture's feasibility. A typical Architecture Vision deliverable will include:

- A problem description and detailed objectives.
- Environment and process models, covering process descriptions and the mapping of process steps to the environment and people.
- Details of actors (human and computer), their roles, responsibilities and requirements.
- The resulting architecture model, covering constraints, IT principles and details of how the requirements are mapped to the architecture to show how IT supports the business processes.

Business Drivers, Business Goals and Business Principles

Business drivers, business goals and business principles provide context for the architectural work, by describing and defining the enterprise.

> **Business drivers** are the people, knowledge and conditions (such as market forces) that initiate and support activities for which the business was designed.

> **Business goals**, sometimes referred to as mission statements, are the things that a business hopes to achieve during its time in operation. Profitability is a typical business goal.

> **Business principles** define how a business operates and expresses its core values and behaviours.

Capability Assessment

A capability assessment ensures that the organisation understands the current baseline and target capability levels of the enterprise. This assessment is first carried out in the Architecture Vision Phase A and updated in the Opportunities & Solutions Phase E. There are four types of capability assessment:

1. **Business capability assessment** - identifies the current capability level of the enterprise and defines the architectural focus areas that will support the desired development of the enterprise.
2. **IT capability assessment** - identifies the maturity level of the IT function within the enterprise and what the likely implications of conducting the architecture project in terms of design governance, operational governance, skills and organisational structure. It also identifies what is an appropriate style, level of formality, amount of detail for the architecture project to fit with the culture and capability of the IT organisation.
3. **Architecture maturity assessment** - identifies the capability and maturity of the architecture function within the enterprise and what architectural assets are currently in existence. It also identifies if the existing artefacts are accurate and what standards and reference models need to be considered.
4. **Business transformation readiness assessment** - identifies where capability gaps exist, to what extent the business is ready to transform in order to reach the target capability given the existing

capability gaps. It identifies what other risks to transformation, cultural barriers and other considerations need to be addressed by the project.

Change Request

As the implementation of the architecture progresses, new facts (such as changes in business strategy and new technology opportunities) may become known that mean the current architecture definition and requirements are no longer suitable or not sufficient to complete the implementation of a solution. A change request may then be submitted in order to request a dispensation or to begin a further cycle of architectural work during the Architecture Change Management Phase H.

Typical contents of a change request are:

- A description of the proposed change, its rationale, and unique reference number.
- An impact assessment of the proposed change.

Communications Plan

Effective communication is a critical success factor for Enterprise Architecture. Development of a communications plan for the architecture in the Architecture Vision Phase allows communications to target information to the right stakeholders, at the right time, via a managed process. Typical contents of a communications plan are:

- Identification of communication needs and requirements for each audience (*who, what*).
- Identification of mechanisms that will be used to communicate with stakeholders, such as meetings, updates and repositories (*how*).
- Identification of a communications timetable (*when*).

Compliance Assessment

Compliance assessments are carried out in the Implementation Governance Phase G and provide a mechanism to review the implementation project's progress to ensure that the design and implementation is inline with the strategic and architectural objectives. Compliance assessments ensure that the Architecture Vision is appropriately realised and that any implementation learning is fed back into the architecture process.

Implementation and Migration Plan

The implementation and migration plan provides details of the projects that will implement the Target Architecture arranged by programmes of work. The plan is initially created in the Opportunities & Solutions Phase E and completed in the Migration Planning Phase F.

Implementation Governance Model

Once the architecture has been developed, it is necessary to plan how the architecture will be governed through its implementation. The Implementation Governance model is produced as an output of the Migration Planning Phase F and typically contains:

- A governance organisation structure with defined roles and responsibilities.
- A governance process, with defined checkpoints and success / failure criteria.

Organisational Model for Enterprise Architecture

The organisational model for Enterprise Architecture ensures that the Architecture Framework is supported by the correct organisation, roles and responsibilities within the enterprise and is an important deliverable from the Preliminary Phase. The organisational model for Enterprise Architecture defines the boundaries between different Enterprise Architecture practitioners and the governance relationships that span across these boundaries. Typical contents of an organisational model for Enterprise Architecture are:

- Scope of organisations impacted.
- Maturity assessment, gaps, and resolution approach.
- Roles and responsibilities for architecture team(s), and the governance and support strategy.
- Constraints on architectural work.
- Budget requirements.

Request for Architectural Work

This is a high-level document sent by the sponsoring organisation to the architecture practice to initiate the start of an Architecture Development Method cycle. Requests for architectural work can be created in one of the following ways:

- As an output of the Preliminary Phase.
- As a result of an approved architecture change request.
- As terms of reference for architectural work originating from Migration Planning.

A request for architectural work will, typically, include:

- Organisation sponsors and a mission statement.
- Business goals, strategic business plans, and changes to the business environment.
- Time constraints, financial constraints, organisation constraints, business constraints and external constraints.
- Descriptions of the current business, IT and architecture.
- Details of available resources.

Requirements Impact Assessment

As the ADM phases progress, new information and facts are collected that may invalidate existing aspects of the architecture. A requirements impact assessment will assess the current architecture requirements and specification to identify changes to the target architecture and the impact of those changes.

Solution Building Blocks

Solution Building Blocks document the implementation-specific building blocks from the enterprise's Architecture Repository.

Statement of Architectural Work

The statement of architectural work is an Architecture Vision Phase A deliverable that defines the scope and approach that will be used to complete an architecture project. The statement of architectural work is used to measure the successful execution of the architecture project and may form the contractual agreement between the supplier and consumer of architecture services. A statement of architectural work will normally contain:

- A statement of work title.
- Details of the project background, description and background.
- The architectural vision.
- The managerial approach and details of the change of scope process.
- Documented responsibilities and deliverables.
- A project plan and schedule.
- Acceptance criteria, procedures and details of signature approvals.

Tailored Architecture Framework

TOGAF provides an industry-standard framework for architecture that can be tailored both to fit the organisation that intends to use it and the type of architecture projects to be undertaken.

The TOGAF model can be tailored to integrate into the enterprise's project and process management frameworks. This may involve customisation of terminology, presentational styles, choice of deployment of architecture tools, as well as enterprise contextual factors, such as culture, stakeholders, commercial concerns and the existing level of Architecture Capability.

Tailoring TOGAF to address the specific architecture projects to be undertaken will involve selecting appropriate deliverables and artefacts to meet project and stakeholder needs. The content of a tailored Architecture Framework will include:

- A tailored architecture method.
- Tailored architecture content.
- Configured and deployed tools.
- Interfaces with governance models and other frameworks.

Transition Architecture

If moving from the Baseline (*as-is*) architecture to the Target (*to-be*) architecture is not to be achieved in one step (say, to provide incremental business benefit) then one or more Transition Architectures (sets of co-ordinated building blocks) will need to be documented to show the transition from Baseline to Target via the Transition Architectures.

Transition Architectures can be used to group incremental functionality into managed programmes that provide business value as the architecture moves from Baseline to Target via the transition architectures. Transition Architectures are outputs from the Opportunities & Solutions Phase E of the ADM.

Exam Preparation Tasks

Review All the Key Topics

Review the most important topics from this chapter listed in table 9 on page 109:

Description	Page
Briefly explain the role of architecture deliverables across the ADM cycle.	103
Explain the purpose of Architecture Building Blocks.	104
Explain the purpose of Architecture Contracts.	104
Explain the purpose of an architecture definition document.	104
Explain the purpose of the Architecture Repository.	104
Explain the purpose of an architecture requirements specification.	104
Explain the purpose of an Architecture Roadmap.	104
Explain the purpose of the Architecture Vision.	104
Explain the purpose of business drivers, business goals and business principles.	105
Explain the purpose of a capability assessment.	105
Explain the purpose of a change request.	106
Explain the purpose of a communications plan.	106
Explain the purpose of a compliance assessment.	106
Explain the purpose of an implementation and migration plan.	106
Explain the purpose of an Implementation Governance Model.	106
Explain the purpose of an organisational model for Enterprise Architecture.	106
Explain the purpose of a request for architectural work.	107
Explain the purpose of a requirements impact assessment.	107
Explain the purpose of Solution Building Blocks.	107
Explain the purpose of a statement of architectural work.	107
Explain the purpose of a tailored Architecture Framework.	108

Table 9: *ADM deliverables exam syllabus checklist*

Understand the Definition of Key Terms

Define the following key terms from this chapter and check your answers:

- Architecture Building Blocks
- Architecture Contracts
- Architecture definition document
- Architecture Principles
- Architecture Repository
- Architecture requirements specification
- Architecture Roadmap
- Architecture Vision
- Business drivers
- Business goals
- Business principles
- Capability assessment

- Change request
- Communications plan
- Compliance assessment
- Implementation and Migration plan
- Implementation Governance model
- Organisational model for Enterprise Architecture
- Request for architectural work
- Requirements impact assessment
- Solution Building Blocks
- Statement of architecture work
- Tailored Architecture Framework
- Transition Architecture

Complete the review questions

Check your understanding of this chapter by answering the following example exam-style questions:

Q1. Which of the following documents acts as the deliverable container for the business, data, application and technology architectural artefacts?   (Select 1)

    A.   Architecture Contract

    B.   Architecture definition document

    C.   Architecture requirements specification

    D.   Architecture Roadmap

    E.   Architecture Vision

Q2. Which of the following are TOGAF architectural deliverables?
(Select 5)

    A.   Architecture Building Blocks and models held in the enterprise's Architecture Repository

    B.   Delivery programme plans and schedules

    C.   Architecture Contracts

    D.   Capability assessments

    E.   A risks, issues, assumptions and dependencies log

    F.   A communications plan

    G.   IT vendor product roadmaps

    H.   Implementation Governance model

Q3. What are the four types of assessments made by an enterprise using TOGAF?
(Select 4)

    A.   Business capability assessment

    B.   Data capability assessment

    C.   Architecture capability assessment

    D.   Information technology (IT) capability assessment

    E.   Architecture maturity assessment

    F.   Security assessment

    G.   Business transformation readiness assessment

Q4. In which phase of the TOGAF ADM are compliance assessments made?
(Select 1)

    A.   Phase A & Phase G

    B.   Phase A to D

    C.   Phase G

    D.   Phase F

    E.   All phases

Q5. Which of the following are **true** for requests for architectural work?
(Select 2)

    A.   They are an output of the Architecture Vision Phase.

    B.   They are an output of the Preliminary Phase or as a result of an approved architecture change request.

    C.   They will typically include details of the organisation sponsors and mission statement.

    D.   They are not concerned with the availability of resources, only the required business needs.

Q6. **What of the following will a tailored Architecture Framework include?**
(Select 4)

    A.   A cost versus benefit analysis of the tailoring activity.

    B.   Tailored architecture method.

    C.   Tailored project management method.

    D.   Tailored architecture content.

    E.   Tailored governance method.

    F.   Configured and deployed tools.

    G.   Interfaces with governance models and other frameworks.

Q7. **Which of the following best describes a Transition Architecture?**
(Select 1)

    A.   The description of a future state ('to-be') of the architecture being developed for an organisation.

    B.   The initial system architecture before a cycle of architecture review and redesign - it can be thought of as the 'as-is' view.

    C.   An architecture stage between the Baseline Architecture and the Target Architecture.

    D.   An architecture showing the logical software and hardware capabilities required to support deployment of business, data and application services.

    E.   A formal description of the enterprise, providing an organising framework for operational and change activity and can also be used as an executive-level, long-term view for direction setting.

Review your answers

Review your answers by referring to the answers that can be found on page 182.

Further Reading and Resources

The following list provides further recommended sources of information for areas covered by this chapter:

- TOGAF 9 Part IV - *Architecture Content Framework*, Chapter 36 (Architecture Deliverables)

This chapter covers the following exam subject:

- Understanding the Guidelines & Techniques that are available to support the application of the TOGAF ADM.

CHAPTER 10

ADM Guidelines & Techniques

The purpose of this chapter of the Study Guide is to enable you to:

- Explain the contents of Part III of TOGAF 9 specification document.
- Explain the need for Architecture Principles and where they are used within the TOGAF ADM.
- Describe the standard template for Architecture Principles.
- Explain what makes a good Architecture Principle.
- Understand what a business scenario is and its purpose.
- Explain where business scenarios are used within the ADM cycle.
- Explain the purpose of gap analysis.
- Describe the gap analysis technique.
- Explain the term 'interoperability'.
- Understand the use of interoperability requirements within the TOGAF ADM.
- Understand the business transformation readiness programme.
- Understand where business transformation readiness is used within the ADM.
- Understand the characteristics of risk management.
- Understand where risk management is used within the TOGAF ADM.
- Understand capability-based planning.

TOGAF 9 Part III Overview

TOGAF 9 Part III contains a collection of Guidelines & Techniques for use in applying the ADM. The guidelines document how to adapt the ADM process, whereas the techniques are used when performing specific tasks in the ADM.

Guidelines for adapting the ADM process include:

- Applying iteration to the ADM.
- Applying the ADM at different enterprise levels.
- Security considerations when applying the ADM.
- Using TOGAF to define and govern Service-Oriented Architectures (SOAs).

The TOGAF 9 Foundation syllabus covers the following sub-set of TOGAF 9 Part III:

- Architecture Patterns.
- Architecture Principles.
- Business scenarios.
- Business transformation readiness assessment.
- Capability-based planning.
- Gap analysis.
- Interoperability requirements.
- Migration planning techniques.

- Risk management.
- Stakeholder management.

Business Scenarios

Delivering business scenarios is a key factor in the success of any major project with the organisation's future depending upon the right outcome. Business Scenarios are a technique used to help identify and understand the business requirements that an architecture must address. Business scenarios are used heavily in the initial ADM Phases (A & B) to define the relevant business requirements and build consensus with stakeholders. A business scenario describes:

- A business process, application, or set of applications.
- The business and technology environment.
- The people and computing components ('actors') who execute the business scenario.
- The desired outcome of proper execution of the scenario.

The Benefits of Developing a Business Scenario

The benefits of developing business scenarios are:

- The business value of solving the problem is clear to all stakeholders.
- A business scenario is a complete description of a business problem, defined in both business and architectural terms.
- They allow the architecture to be based on a complete set of requirements that define a whole-problem description.
- Individual requirements are viewed in relation to one another and in the context of the overall problem.

A Good Business Scenario

A good business scenario is SMART, i.e., it is:

- **Specific**, defines what needs to be done in the business.
- **Measurable**, gives clear metrics for success.
- **Actionable**, clearly defines the problem and provides details of the solution.
- **Realistic**, shows the problem can be solved within the bounds of the resource constraints.
- **Time-bound**, has a clear statement of when the opportunity expires.

Building a Business Scenario

The technique may be used iteratively and at different levels of detail in the hierarchical decomposition of the Business Architecture. Figure 14 on page 115 shows an overview of the generic business scenario process.

114

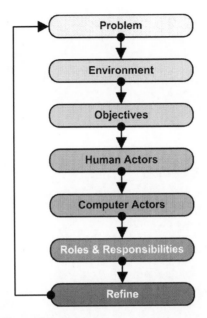

Figure 14: *The business scenario process*

The business scenario process shown in Figure 14 is as follows:

1. Identify the **problem**, document and rank the problem that is driving the scenario.
2. Identify the business and technical **environments** where the problem situation is occurring.
3. Identify and document (in a SMART way) the desired **objectives**; the results of handling the problems successfully.
4. Identify **human actors**, their place in the business model, and their roles.
5. Identify **computer actors**, their place in the technology model, the computing elements and their roles.
6. Identify and document **roles, responsibilities** and measures of success per actor, and the desired results of handling the situation properly.
7. Check for 'fitness-for-purpose' and **refine** by iteration if necessary.

Business Scenarios within the ADM cycle

Business requirements are important throughout all phases of the ADM cycle. The business scenario technique has an important role to play in the TOGAF ADM by ensuring that the business requirements themselves are complete and correct.

Business scenarios figure most prominently in the initial phase of the ADM, especially during the Architecture Vision Phase A when they are used to define relevant business requirements and to build consensus with stakeholders. Business scenarios may also be used in other phases to derive the characteristics of the architecture directly from the high-level requirements of the business.

Gap Analysis

The gap analysis technique is used in the ADM to validate an architecture by comparing the Baseline Architecture with the Target Architecture. A gap analysis can be used to consider what may have been missed in the architectural design such as a stakeholder's concerns that have not been addressed. Potential gaps include:

- Business domain:
  - People gaps (e.g., cross-training requirements).
  - Process gaps (e.g., process inefficiencies).

- Tool gaps (e.g., duplicate or missing tool functionality).

- Information gaps.

- Measurement gaps.

- Financial gaps.

- Facilities gaps (e.g., buildings, office space).

- Data domain:

  - Data is stale and out-of-date.

  - Data is not located where it is needed.

  - Data is not available when needed.

  - Data does not exist or is incomplete.

  - Data is created / stored but not used.

  - There are data relationship gaps.

- Application domain:

  - Applications are impacted on, eliminated, or created.

- Technology domain:

  - Technologies are impacted on, eliminated, or created.

The Gap Analysis Technique

A gap analysis can be carried out by drawing up a matrix with all the Architecture Building Blocks (ABB) of the Baseline Architecture on the vertical axis and all the Architecture Building Blocks of the Target Architecture on the horizontal axis. Figure 15 on page 117 shows an example gap analysis diagram.

An additional row labelled 'New Services' is added and to the Target Architecture axis a final column labelled 'Eliminated Services'. Where a service (ABB) is available in both the Baseline and Target Architectures, this is recorded with the value 'Included' in the intersecting cell. Where a service from the Baseline Architecture is missing in the Target Architecture, it must be reviewed. If the services were correctly eliminated it is marked as such in the appropriate 'Eliminated Services' cell. If they were not, then an accidental omission has been uncovered in the Target Architecture that must be addressed by reinstating the services in the next iteration of the architecture design.

If a service from the Target Architecture cannot be found in the Baseline Architecture, then this service will need to be developed or procured.

Baseline Architecture	Target Architecture			Eliminated Services
	Data Encryption Services	Large Format Colour Printing	Desktop Publishing Services	
Email Services				Intentionally Eliminated
Data Encryption Services	Partial Match			
Large Format Colour Printing		Included		
Remote Access Services				Missing – a gap in the Target Architecture
New Sevices	Gap: Enhanced Encryption Services		Gap: Service to be produced	

Figure 15: *A gap analysis example*

The gap analysis technique can be used in Phases B to E of the ADM.

Interoperability

TOGAF defines interoperability as, 'the ability to share information and services'. Defining the degree that information and services are to be shared is very important, and a key objective of an Enterprise Architecture is to define interoperability in a clear and unambiguous manner. Interoperability can be defined as:

- The ability to share information and services.
- The ability for two or more systems / components to exchange and use the same information.
- The ability for systems to provide services and consume services of other systems so as to operate effectively together.

Interoperability Requirements within the TOGAF ADM

The determination of interoperability occurs throughout the ADM:

- In Phase A - Architectural Vision, the nature and security considerations of information and service exchanges are found in the business scenarios.
- In Phase B - Business Architecture, information and service exchanges are defined in business terms.
- In Phase C – Information Systems Data Architecture, the content of information exchanges is detailed using the corporate data and/or information exchange model.
- In Phase C – Information Systems Application Architecture, how applications will share information and services is specified.
- In Phase D - Technology Architecture, the technology to permit information and service exchanges are specified.
- In Phase E - Opportunities & Solutions, actual solutions are selected for implementation.

117

- In Phase F - Migration Planning, interoperability is implemented through the delivery of the Target Architecture.

Interoperability Categorised

Interoperability can be categorised as follows:

- Operational or business interoperability defines how business processes are to be shared.
- Information interoperability defines how information is to be shared between systems.
- Technical interoperability defines how technical services are to be shared or at least connected to one another. From an IT perspective, technical interoperability can be further broken down as follows:

  - Presentation integration / interoperability is where a common look-and-feel approach is required.

  - Information integration / interoperability is where the corporate information is seamlessly shared. An example is single sign-on where one set of security credentials can be used to access multiple systems.

  - Application integration / interoperability is where the corporate functionality is integrated and shareable so that the applications are not duplicated.

  - Technical integration / interoperability includes common methods and shared services for the communication, storage, processing and access to data primarily in the application platform and communications infrastructure domains.

Business Transformation

Enterprise Architecture often involves considerable change at multiple levels. A business transformation readiness assessment provides a technique for understanding the readiness of an organisation to accept change, identifying the issues and dealing with them in the migration plan.

Most organisations will have their own unique set of factors, but the majority will be similar to other organisations. Example factors are:

- **Vision** - the ability to clearly define and communicate the desired change.
- **Desire**, **willingness** and **resolve** - the presence of a desire to achieve the results and overcome any difficulties that arise.
- **Need** - the compelling need to achieve the desired change.

Business Transformation Readiness within the ADM

An initial assessment of business transformation readiness is carried out in the Architecture Vision Phase A to evaluate and quantify an organisation's readiness to undergo change. Phase A also includes an assessment as a scoping activity. Later, in Phases E & F are an assessment and evaluation done as part of the planning activity as a joint effort between corporate staff, lines of business and IT planners.

Determining the Readiness Factors

- The ability to define and communicate what is to be achieved.
- The desire to achieve the results and a compelling need.
- A business case, funding, sponsorship and leadership.
- Governance and accountability.
- Workable approach and execution model.
- IT capability to execute, and an enterprise with an ability to implement and operate.

Present Readiness Factors

- Assess the current maturity level.
- Determine the target maturity level.
- Determine achievable intermediate targets.

Assess Readiness Factors

- Readiness factor vision - an understanding of where the organisation needs to evolve to.
- Readiness factor rating - based on the degrees of urgency, the readiness state and the degrees of difficulty.

Assess Risks

- Derive a set of actions to ensure a change to an acceptable state.
- Assess with respect to risk.
- Identify mitigating actions.

Integrate Actions into Plans

- Integrate the required actions into implementation plans in ADM Phases E and F.

Risk Management

Risk management is documented in TOGAF 9 Part III - ADM Guidelines & Techniques, Chapter 31 (Risk Management) and is a technique used to mitigate risk when implementing an architecture project.

There are two levels of risk that need to be considered in risk management:

1. **Initial level of risk** - risk prior to determining and implementing mitigating actions.
2. **Residual level of risk** - risk after implementation of mitigating actions.

Criteria for Risk Assessment

Measuring the effect and frequency of risk has no set rules. However, the best practices for risk management provide the following criteria to be used in assessments.

For effect:

- **Catastrophic** - critical financial loss that has the possibility of causing the enterprise to become bankrupt.
- **Critical** - serious financial loss in more than one area of the business and a loss in productivity.
- **Marginal** - financial loss in a single area of the business and a reduced return on the IT investment.
- **Negligible** - minimal impact on a single area of the business affecting its ability to deliver products or services.

For frequency:

- **Frequent** - likely to occur often or continuously.
- **Likely** - occurs several times during a transformation cycle.
- **Occasional** - occurs sporadically.
- **Seldom** - remote possibility that it will occur.
- **Unlikely** - will not occur.

Recommended Process

The recommended process for managing risk consists of the following activities:

- **Risk classification** - classifying risk based on time, cost, scope, client relationship impact, contractual, technological, complexity, corporate, personnel and client acceptance.
- **Risk identification** - risks identified so that a suitable strategy (Capability Maturity Models, Business Transformation Readiness, Prince 2 & PMBOK) can be used to address them.
- **Initial risk assessment** - risks classified in two dimensions by **effect**, such as catastrophic, critical, marginal or negligible and **frequency**, such as frequent, likely, occasional, seldom, unlikely.
- **Risk mitigation and residual risk assessment** - using the two classification dimensions, the intersection of each risk can then be defined as one of the following classifications: extremely high risk, high risk, moderate risk or low risk.
- **Risk monitoring** - residual risk needs to be approved as part of the governance framework to ensure that the mitigation actions are carried out and monitored.

Risk Management within the TOGAF ADM

Risk exists in all Enterprise Architecture activity and is identified in all phases within the ADM. In the Architecture Vision Phase A, risks are classified, identified, assessed and risk mitigation activities included in the statement of architectural work. In Phase G (Implementation Governance), risk monitoring is conducted. Implementation Governance can identify critical risks not being mitigated and might require another full or partial ADM cycle.

Capability-Based Planning

A capability is an ability that an organisation, person or system possesses. Capability-based planning is a business-planning technique that focuses on business outcomes. The attributes of the technique are:

- It addresses planning, engineering and delivery of strategic business capabilities.
- The benefits accrue to the enterprise as a whole, rather than to specific units. In fact, specific units may actually be negatively impacted on.
- The planning requires the ability to cross organisational boundaries.
- The process is business-driven and business-led.

Figure 16 below, illustrates the relationship between capability-based planning, Enterprise Architecture and portfolio / project management:

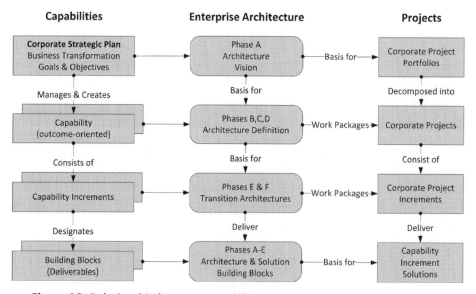

Figure 16: *Relationship between capabilities, Enterprise Architecture & projects*

Some capabilities can be handled within the context of a business organisation structure; however, most capabilities are 'horizontal' and cut across the vertical segmentation of most corporate governance.

Capability-based planning and Enterprise Architecture are mutually supportive and both cut across vertical segmentation of organisations.

Exam Preparation Tasks

Review All the Key Topics

Review the most important topics from this chapter listed in table 10 below:

Description	Page
Briefly explain the contents of Part III of TOGAF 9.	113
Understand what a business scenario is and its purpose.	116
Explain where business scenarios are used within the ADM cycle.	115
Explain the purpose of a gap analysis.	115
Describe the gap analysis technique.	116
Explain the term 'interoperability'.	117
Understand the use of interoperability requirements within the TOGAF ADM.	117
Understand the business transformation readiness programme.	118
Understand where business transformation readiness is used within the ADM.	118
Understand the characteristics of risk management.	119
Understand where risk management is used within the TOGAF ADM.	120
Understand capability-based planning.	120

Table 10: *ADM Guidelines & Techniques exam syllabus checklist*

Understand the Definition of Key Terms

Define the following key terms from this chapter and check your answers:

- Architecture Principles
- Architecture Patterns
- Business scenarios
- Business transformation
- Business transformation readiness assessment

- Capability-based planning
- Gap analysis
- Interoperability requirements
- Migration planning techniques
- Risk management
- Stakeholder management

Complete the Review Questions

Check your understanding of this chapter by answering the following example exam-style questions:

Q1. **Which of the following are contained in Part III of TOGAF 9?**
(Select 5)
A. Business scenarios
B. Risk management
C. Entity-relationship modelling
D. Capability-based planning
E. Re-factoring
F. SCAMPI Assessments
G. Gap analysis
H. Interoperability requirements

Q2. What are business scenarios?
(Select 1)

A. Business scenarios are a technique used to help identify and understand the business requirements that an architecture must address.

B. Business scenarios are a technique used to classify risk based on time, cost, scope, client relationship impact, contractual, technological, complexity, corporate, personnel and client acceptance.

C. Business scenarios provide the ability to clearly define and communicate the desired change.

D. Business scenarios define how technical services are to be shared or at least connect to one another.

E. Business scenarios are widely used in the ADM to validate an architecture that is being developed by comparing the baseline architecture with the target architecture.

Q3. Which main ADM Phases are business scenarios normally generated?
(Select 1)

A. Phases A & B

B. Phases B & C

C. Phases C & D

D. Phases D & E

E. Phases G & H

F. Preliminary Phase & Phase A

Q4. What does the acronym 'SMART' stand for with respect to business scenarios?
(Select 1)

A. Sufficient, meaningful, articulate, realistic and time-bound.

B. Specific, meaningful, actionable, realistic and time-bound.

C. Sufficient, meaningful, actionable, realistic and time-bound.

D. Specific, measurable, actionable, realistic and time-bound.

E. Specific, meaningful, actionable, realistic and time-bound.

Q5. What is the usual purpose of gap analysis in TOGAF?
(Select 1)

A. To validate an architecture that is being developed by comparing the baseline architecture with the Data Architecture.

B. To mitigate risk when implementing an architecture project by comparing the requirements document with the Baseline Architecture.

C. To validate an architecture that is being developed by comparing the Baseline Architecture with the Target Architecture.

D. To validate an architecture that is being developed by comparing the Baseline Architecture with the Technology Architecture.

E. To mitigate risk when implementing an architecture project by comparing the requirements document with the Data Architecture.

Q6. Which of the following statements best defines the term 'interoperability' in TOGAF 9?
(Select 1)

A. The ability to share information and services.

B. The ability to share data between systems.

C. The ability for one system to consume data from another system.

D. For two or more systems to use the same data schema.

E. For two or more systems to use the same technology stack.

Q7. The determination of interoperability occurs throughout the ADM; which of the following statements are correct?   (Select 3)

  A. In the Preliminary Phase, the nature and security considerations of information and service exchanges are found in the business scenarios.
  B. In Phase A - Architecture Vision, the nature and security considerations of information and service exchanges are found in the business scenarios.
  C. In Phase C - Business Architecture, information and service exchanges are defined in business terms.
  D. In Phase B - Business Architecture, information and service exchanges are defined in business terms.
  E. In Phase C - Data Architecture, information and service exchanges are defined in business terms.
  F. In Phase C - Data Architecture, the content of information exchanges is detailed using the corporate data and/or information exchange model.
  G. In Phase F - Migration Planning, interoperability is implemented logically.
  H. In Phase F - Migration Planning, interoperability is implemented physically.

Q8. What is the business transformation readiness programme?
(Select 1)

  A. The process of validating an architecture that is being developed by comparing the Baseline Architecture with the Data Architecture.
  B. A technique used to help identify and understand the business requirements that an architecture must address.
  C. A business planning technique that focuses on business outcomes.
  D. The practice and orientation by which Enterprise Architecture and other architectures are managed and controlled at an enterprise-wide level.
  E. A technique for understanding if an organisation is ready to accept change, identifying the issues and dealing with them in the implementation and migration plan.

Q9. In which ADM Phase or Phases would a business transformation readiness assessment be used?
(Select 1)

  A. Phase A
  B. Phase F
  C. Phases E & F
  D. Phases A, E & F
  E. Phases A & F
  F. All ADM Phases

Q10. What are the recommended process steps for managing risk?
(Select 1)

  A. Classification, identification, assessment and elimination.
  B. Classification, identification, assessment, mitigation and monitoring.
  C. Identification, classification, mitigation and monitoring.
  D. Assessment, mitigation and monitoring.
  E. Classification, identification, assessment, mitigation, elimination and monitoring.

Q11. What is capability-based planning?
(Select 1)

A. The process of validating an architecture that is being developed by comparing the Baseline Architecture with the Data Architecture.

B. A technique used to help identify and understand the business requirements that an architecture must address.

C. A business planning technique that focuses on business outcomes.

D. The practice and orientation by which Enterprise Architecture and other architectures are managed and controlled at an enterprise-wide level.

E. A technique for understanding the readiness of an organisation to accept change, identifying the issues and dealing with them in the implementation and migration plan.

Q12. Which of the following are attributes of capability-based planning?
(Select 3)

A. It addresses planning, engineering and delivery of strategic business capabilities.

B. The benefits accrue to the enterprise as a whole, rather than to specific units. In fact, specific units may actually be negatively impacted on.

C. The planning does not require the need to cross organisational boundaries.

D. The planning requires the ability to cross organisational boundaries.

E. The benefits may accrue to specific units, rather than to the enterprise as a whole. The enterprise may actually be negatively impacted on unless care is taken.

Q13. What is residual risk?
(Select 1)

A. Risk with a sufficiently low probability and minimal impact that it can be ignored.

B. Risk from not implementing the Target Architecture correctly.

C. Risk categorisation after implementation of mitigating actions.

D. Risk that can never be mitigated against.

E. Risk that any mitigating actions would be too costly to the organisation to implement.

Review Your Answers

Review your answers by referring to the answers that can be found on page 182.

Further Reading and Resources

The following list provides further recommended sources of information for areas covered by this chapter:

- TOGAF 9 Part III - *ADM Guidelines & Techniques*, Chapter 18 (Introduction)
- TOGAF 9 Part III - *ADM Guidelines & Techniques*, Chapter 23 (Architecture Principles)
- TOGAF 9 Part III - *ADM Guidelines & Techniques*, Chapter 26 (Business Scenarios)
- TOGAF 9 Part III - *ADM Guidelines & Techniques*, Chapter 27 (Gap Analysis)
- TOGAF 9 Part III - *ADM Guidelines & Techniques*, Chapter 29 (Interoperability Requirements)
- TOGAF 9 Part III - *ADM Guidelines & Techniques*, Chapter 30 (Business Transformation Readiness Assessment)
- TOGAF 9 Part III - *ADM Guidelines & Techniques*, Chapter 31 (Risk Management)
- TOGAF 9 Part III - *ADM Guidelines & Techniques*, Chapter 32 (Capability-Based Planning)

This chapter covers the following exam subjects:

- The Enterprise Continuum.
- The Architecture Continuum.
- The Solutions Continuum.
- The Architecture Repository.
- The three levels of the Architecture Landscape.
- The High-level issues with Tools Standardisation.

CHAPTER 11

Enterprise Continuum & Tools

The purpose of this chapter of the Study Guide is to enable you to:

- Explain the Enterprise Continuum, its purpose and its constituent parts.
- Explain how the Enterprise Continuum is used to organise and develop an architecture and how the Enterprise Continuum promotes the reuse of architecture artefacts.
- Explain the purpose of the Architecture Continuum and its key stages.
- Explain the purpose of the Solutions Continuum, its key stages, and how an architecture evolves through the Solutions Continuum.
- Explain the relationships between the Enterprise Continuum and the TOGAF ADM.
- Describe the Architecture Repository and the relationships between it and the Enterprise Continuum.
- Describe the classes of information held in the Architecture Repository.
- List the three levels of the Architecture Landscape.
- Explain the purpose of the Standards Information Base within the Architecture Repository.
- Explain the high-level issues with tool standardisation.

The Enterprise Continuum

The Enterprise Continuum is a view of the Architecture Repository that classifies the architecture and solution artefacts as they evolve from generic architectures to organisation-specific architectures, or from generic solutions to organisation-specific solutions.

What is the Purpose of the Enterprise Continuum?

The Enterprise Continuum is a *virtual repository* for architecture assets such as models, patterns, architecture descriptions and other artefacts.

The Enterprise Continuum enables the classification of reusable architecture assets / solution assets, and can be thought of as a view of the Architecture Repository. The Enterprise Continuum is used to aid communication between all architects involved in building and procuring the architecture by providing a common language and terminology.

What are the Constituent Parts of the Enterprise Continuum?

A pictorial view of the Enterprise Continuum is shown in figure 17 below:

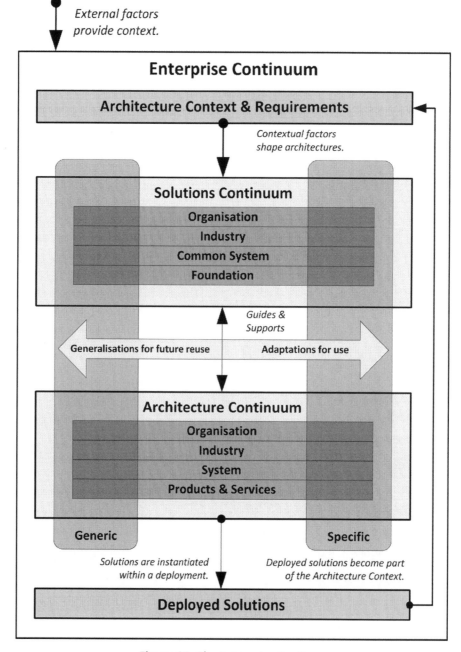

Figure 17: *The Enterprise Continuum*

The Enterprise Continuum consists of three main parts as described below. Each of the three parts is considered to be a distinct continuum.

The Enterprise Continuum

The Enterprise Continuum shows the context for how generic solutions can be leveraged and specialised in order to support the requirements of an individual organisation. The Enterprise Continuum comprises the Architecture Continuum and the Solutions Continuum.

The Solutions Continuum

The Solutions Continuum describes the implementation of the assets defined in the Architecture Continuum. The Solutions Continuum represents an available collection of reusable Solution Building Blocks that implement Architecture Building Blocks defined in the Architecture Continuum.

The Architecture Continuum

The Architecture Continuum defines the generic rules, representations and relationships in an architecture. The Architecture Continuum represents a structure of Architecture Building Blocks used to guide the development and selection of Solution Building Blocks.

How the Enterprise Continuum is Used to Organise and Develop an Architecture

The Enterprise Continuum is a view of the Architecture Repository for classifying architecture and solution artefacts as they evolve from generic Foundation Architectures to Organisation-Specific Architectures. Any architecture is context-specific and so the Enterprise Continuum is valuable because it provides a consistent language to understand and articulate differences between architectures. The Enterprise Continuum aids in understanding, both within individual enterprises and between customer and vendor organisations.

How the Enterprise Continuum Promotes Reuse of Architecture Artefacts

The Enterprise Continuum provides an aid to organising reusable architecture and solution assets and acts as a *virtual repository* that consists of all the architecture assets (such as models, patterns, and architecture descriptions) and other artefacts produced during the ADM Phases.

The Enterprise Continuum can hold both internal (architecture and solution) artefacts and external (architecture and solution) artefacts. External architecture and solution artefacts include Industry Reference Models and Architecture Patterns such as:

- TOGAF's Technical Reference Model (TRM).
- Artefacts specific to certain aspects of IT, such as security architecture.
- Artefacts specific to specific types of information processing such as eBusiness.
- Artefacts specific to certain vertical industries, such as the TMF (in the telecommunications sector) and ARTS (in the retail sector).

The Enterprise Architecture determines which architecture and solution artefacts an organisation includes in its Architecture Repository, with reuse being a major consideration.

Relationships between the Enterprise Continuum and the TOGAF ADM

The TOGAF Architecture Development Method describes the process of moving from the level of Foundation Architecture to an Enterprise-Specific Architecture using the TOGAF Foundation Architecture and other relevant architecture assets, components and building blocks.

There are reminders for architects at various stages within the TOGAF Architecture Development Method to consider which architecture assets from the Enterprise Continuum they should use. TOGAF itself provides two reference models for inclusion in the Enterprise Continuum:

1. The TOGAF Technical Reference Model (TRM) Foundation Architecture. This is covered in more detail on page 157.
2. The TOGAF Integrated Information Infrastructure Reference Model (III-RM). This is covered in more detail on page 161.

The Architecture Continuum

The Architecture Continuum is part of an organisation's Enterprise Continuum and is supported by the Solutions Continuum. The Architecture Continuum represents Architecture Building Blocks that evolve through their development lifecycle from abstract and generic entities to organisation-specific architecture assets. The Architecture Continuum assets are used to guide and select the elements in the Solutions Continuum.

The Architecture Continuum is a useful tool because it allows the architect to identify commonality and eliminate unnecessary redundancy. The Architecture Continuum also shows the relationships between:

- Enterprise Architecture.
- Foundational Frameworks (such as TOGAF).
- Common Systems Architectures (such as the TOGAF III-RM).
- Industry Architectures.

The Architecture Continuum offers a way to define and understand the generic rules, representations and relationships in an information system and it represents a conceptual structuring of reusable architecture assets, which can then be realised by Solution Building Blocks.

What is the Purpose of the Architecture Continuum?

Figure 18 below shows an overview of the TOGAF Architecture Continuum:

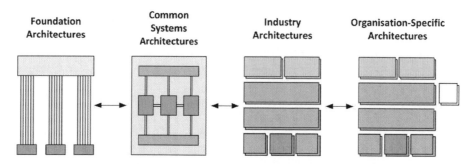

Figure 18: *TOGAF Architecture Continuum overview*

The Architecture Continuum contains reusable Architecture Building Blocks that can be classified into four types.

1. Foundation Architectures

A Foundation Architecture is an architecture of building blocks and corresponding standards that supports generic services and functions to provide a foundation on which more specific architectures and architectural components can be built.

2. Common Systems Architectures

Common Systems Architectures guide the selection and integration of specific services from the Foundation Architecture to create an architecture useful for building common (supporting reuse) solutions across a wide number of relevant domains. Examples of Common Systems Architectures include:

- Security architectures.
- Management architectures.
- Network architectures.
- Operations architectures.

The TOGAF Integrated Information Infrastructure Reference Model (III-RM) is an example of a Common Systems Architecture.

3. *Industry Architectures*

Industry Architectures are used to address specific customer problems within a particular vertical industry domain and to guide the integration of common systems components with industry-specific components. An example industry architecture would be the 'BAIN' architecture that defines a *Banking Industry Architecture Network*.

4. *Organisation-Specific Architectures*

Organisation-Specific Architectures describe and guide the user-developed or third-party components that form the solutions for particular enterprises and have the following characteristics:

- They define the building blocks and reflect the requirements specific to a particular enterprise.
- They encourage implementation of appropriate solutions to meet the needs of the business and provide the criteria to measure and select appropriate products, solutions and services.
- They contain the organisation-specific business models, data, applications and technologies and provide an evolutionary path to support growth and new business needs.
- They provide a means to communicate and manage business operations across all four architectural domains and an evolutionary path to support growth and new business needs.

Key stages in the Architecture Continuum

Figure 18 on page 130 shows the different architectures, from Foundation Architectures (on the left) through to Common Systems Architectures, Industry Architectures and finally Organisation-Specific Architectures (on the right) developed by the organisation itself.

The four different architectures (Foundation, Common System, Industry and Organisation-Specific) guide and support the corresponding solutions. Architectures on the right of Figure 18 focus on meeting enterprise needs and business requirements, while the architectures on the left focus on architectural components and building blocks that can be leveraged.

The enterprise needs and business requirements are addressed in increasing detail from Foundation Architectures through to Organisation-Specific Architectures. The TOGAF architect will find reusable architectural elements toward the left of the Architecture Continuum (Foundation, Common-Systems and Industry) and reusable Architecture Building Blocks - the models of architectures on the right.

The Architecture Continuum and the Solutions Continuum

The Architecture Continuum's relationship with the Solutions Continuum is one of guidance, direction and support. The Foundation Architectures guide the creation or selection of Foundation Solutions. Foundation Solutions, in turn, support the Foundation Architecture by realising the architecture defined in the Architecture Continuum.

The Foundation Architecture also guides the development of Foundation Solutions, by providing architectural direction, requirements and principles. The Foundation Architecture guides the realisation of appropriate solutions. A similar relationship exists between the Common Systems, Industry and Organisation-Specific Architectures of the Enterprise Continuum.

The relationships depicted in figure 19 on page 132 are a best case of architecture and solution components:

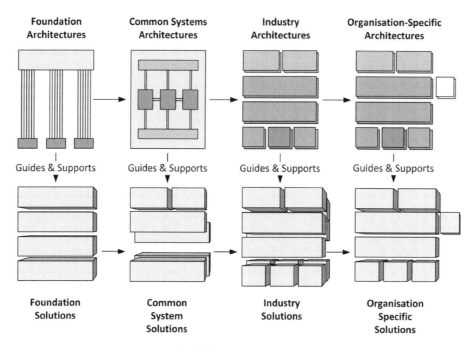

Figure 19: *Architecture Continuum & Solutions Continuum*

The Solutions Continuum

The Solutions Continuum is part of an organisation's Enterprise Continuum and provides a consistent way to describe and understand the implementation of the assets defined in the Architecture Continuum. The Solutions Continuum defines what is available in the organisational environment as reusable Solution Building Blocks that implement the Architecture Building Blocks.

Solution Building Blocks represent implementations of the architectures at corresponding levels of the Architecture Continuum consisting of purchased products or built components that represent a solution to the enterprise's business needs.

What is the Purpose of the Solutions Continuum?

The Solutions Continuum defines what is available in the organisational environment as reusable Solution Building Blocks. The Solutions Continuum is shown in figure 20 below and represents the implementations of the architectures at the corresponding levels of the Architecture Continuum.

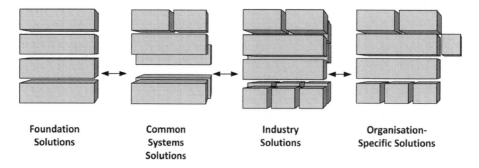

Figure 20: *TOGAF Solution Continuum overview*

At each level in the Solutions Continuum, there is a set of reference building blocks that represent a solution to the business requirements. A Solutions Continuum can be regarded as a reuse repository.

In Figure 20 on the previous page, as we move from left to right, the products and services increase in value as they become Systems Solutions. Systems solutions are used to create Industry Solutions; Industry Solutions are then used to create Enterprise Solutions (also called customer solutions).

What are the Key Stages of the Solutions Continuum?

The Solutions Continuum contains the following solution types:

Foundation Solutions

Foundation Solutions consist of generic tools, products, services and solution components that provide capabilities. Services can cover such items as consulting and training to ensure that the business benefit from the IT investment can be realised as soon as possible. Support services include such services as a help desk or software management systems and are critical in ensuring that the value from the other solutions is realised.

Foundation Solutions include such things as operating systems, programming languages, organisational structures and foundational structures for organising IT operations (such as ITIL).

Common Systems Solutions

A Common Systems Solution is an implementation of a Common Systems Architecture. Common Systems Solutions represent collections of common requirements and capabilities, rather than those specific to a particular customer or industry. Common Systems Solutions provide organisations with operating environments for operational and informational needs, such as high-availability transaction processing and scalable data warehousing systems.

A Common Systems Solution is comprised of a set of products and services, some of which may be certified or branded. Examples of Common Systems Solutions include: web server products, relational database management systems, and messaging middleware.

These Common Systems Solution will normally fall into three categories:

1. Systems vendors, typically providing the technology-centric solution components such a website hosting or managed storage space.
2. 'Software as a service' vendors, providing common application solutions such as email.
3. Business process outsourcing vendors, providing business capability-centric Common Systems Solutions such as project management tools and human resources services.

Industry Solutions

An Industry Solution is an implementation of an Industry Architecture, which provides packages of common components and services specific to an industry that can be reused. Industry Solutions are by their nature industry-specific, ready to be tailored to an individual organisation's requirements. An Industry Solution may include other solution elements, such as specific products, services and Systems Solutions appropriate to that industry. The Industry Solutions are underpinned by Common Systems Solutions and Foundation Solutions.

An example Industry Solution would be a physical database schema for a specific vertical market. An Industry Solution may include specific products, services and Systems Solutions appropriate to that industry. For example, a dental booking system would be an Industry Solution.

Organisation-Specific Solutions

An Organisation Specific Solution is an implementation of an Organisation Specific Architecture. An Organisation Specific Solution provides the required business functionality because it will have been designed for specific business operations to accommodate the people and processes of a specific organisation. Organisation-Specific Solutions leverage and build upon Industry Solutions, Common Systems Solutions and Foundation Solutions.

An Organisation-Specific Solution should define the required operating parameters and quality metrics so that these can be used to monitor and manage the environment. These metrics can then be used to support service-level agreements to ensure the operational systems operate at the desired service levels required by the organisation.

The Architecture Repository

The Architecture Repository supports the Enterprise Continuum and stores different classes of architectural output at different levels of abstraction. An overview of the TOGAF Architecture Repository is shown in figure 21 below:

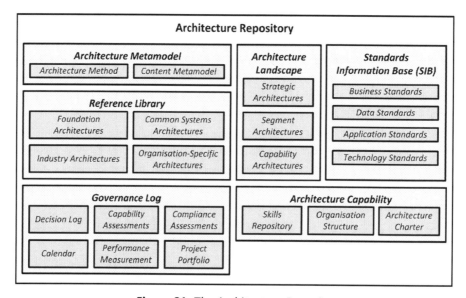

Figure 21: *The Architecture Repository*

What is the Architecture Repository?

An architecture practice in a large enterprise can generate a large volume of architectural artefacts. The effective management of these artefacts requires that the organisation:

- use a formal taxonomy for different types of architectural asset.
- has dedicated processes and tools for architectural content storage.

In addition, the Architecture Repository is part of the enterprise IT repository, which links architectural assets to other repositories containing components such as detailed designs, deployment details and service management.

TOGAF provides a framework for an Architecture Repository that allows an enterprise to identify the different types of architectural assets at different levels of abstraction in the organisation.

What is the purpose of the Architecture Repository?

The purpose of the Architecture Repository is to provide a physical repository that contains a framework for managing architectural work products and is a model of the physical instance of the Enterprise Continuum.

The Classes of Information Held in the Architecture Repository

The Architecture Repository holds six classes of architectural information:

1. Architectural Metamodel

An architecture metamodel defines a formal structure for architectural work products and artefacts to ensure consistency within the Architecture Development Method and provides guidance for organisations that wish to implement their architecture within a tool.

2. Architecture Capability

Defines the parameters, structures and processes that support the governance of the Architecture Repository to realise the business vision.

3. Architecture Landscape

The Architecture Landscape shows an architectural view of the building blocks (live) in use within the organisation. The landscape will be defined at multiple levels of granularity to suit different architecture objectives. Normally, three levels of granularity are defined: Strategic Architectures, Segmented Architectures and Capability Architectures.

4. Standards Information Base (SIB)

Stores details of the standards with which all new architectures must comply. It is a database of facts and holds details of industry standards, selected products and services from suppliers, shared services already deployed within the organisation or formal standards bodies.

5. Reference Library

The Reference Library provides templates, patterns, guidelines and other reference material useful in the creation of new architectures for the enterprise. The Reference Library holds the contents of the Enterprise Continuum.

6. Governance Log

The Governance Log provides a record of governance activity that has taken place across the enterprise and provides a repository area to hold shared information relating to the on-going governance of projects.

The Purpose of the Standards Information Base within the Architecture Repository

The Standards Information Base is a repository area that can hold a set of specifications, to which architectures must conform. Establishing a Standards Information Base assists in the Architecture Governance process by:

- Providing standards easily accessible to projects, so that the projects' obligations can be understood and planned for.
- Providing standards stated in a clear and unambiguous manner, so that compliance can be objectively assessed.

The Standards Information Base may include approved products, industry standards, services from suppliers or services already deployed in the organisation that can be leveraged.

The Relationship between the Enterprise Continuum and the Architecture Repository

The Enterprise Continuum is a view of the repository that contains all the architectural assets i.e., architecture descriptions, models, building blocks, patterns, viewpoints and other artefacts that make up the Enterprise Architecture.

The Enterprise Architecture, in turn, determines which architecture and solution artefacts an organisation includes in its Architecture Repository with reuse being a major consideration.

The Three Levels of the Architecture Landscape

The Architecture Landscape contains architectural views of the state of the enterprise at particular points in time. Figure 22 below illustrates the Architecture Landscape and how it can be used to partition architectural activity.

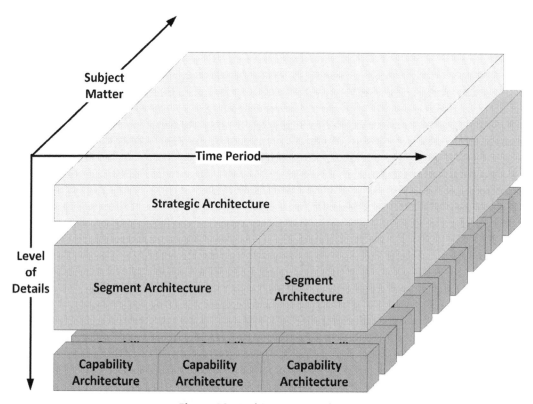

Figure 22: *Architecture Landscape*

The Architecture Landscape is divided into three levels of granularity:

Strategic Architectures

Strategic Architectures show a summary view of the entire enterprise over a long period of time. They provide a framework for direction at an executive level and support change activity at the operational level.

Segment Architectures

Segment Architectures provide a formal, more detailed description of operating models for areas within an enterprise. They can be used at the programme level to organise and align specific change activities operationally.

Capability Architectures

A Capability Architecture is a highly-detailed description of the architectural approach to realise a particular solution. They are used to provide an overview of current capability, details of the target capability, capability increments, and allow for individual work packages to be grouped within managed portfolios and programmes. These programmes will move the enterprise from its current capability through the capability increments to the target capability.

The High-Level Issues with Tools Standardisation

The contents of the Enterprise Continuum need to be managed and tools are, therefore, needed to:

- Allow the architecture information contained in the Enterprise Continuum to be shared within the organisation.
- Ensure that the artefacts in the Enterprise Continuum use a common and consistent terminology.
- Promote the reuse of artefacts.
- Reduce the burden of maintaining the architecture.
- Provide stakeholders with the relevant models that reflect their areas of concern by supporting enquiries for models, views and other queries.

Key Issues in Tools Standardisation

There are two key issues in tools standardisation:

1. The choice of a single 'one size fits all' tool versus multiple 'best of breed' tools.
2. The ability of a single tool to address all needs and at all levels of maturity.

TOGAF recognises the complexity in tools standardisation, and provides a set of evaluation criteria and guidelines for an organisation selecting suitable tools.

Exam Preparation Tasks

Review All the key topics

Review the most important topics from this chapter listed in table 11 on page 137:

Description	Page
Briefly explain what the Enterprise Continuum is.	127
Explain how the Enterprise Continuum is used to organise and develop an architecture.	129
Explain how the Enterprise Continuum promotes re-use of architecture artefacts.	129
Describe the constituent parts of the Enterprise Continuum.	128
Explain the purpose of the Enterprise Continuum.	127
Explain the purpose of the Architecture Continuum.	130
List the stages of architecture evolution defined in the Architecture Continuum.	131
Explain the purpose of the Solutions Continuum.	132
List the stages of architecture evolution defined in the Solutions Continuum.	133
Explain the relationship between the Enterprise Continuum and the TOGAF ADM.	135
Describe the Architecture Repository.	134
Explain the relationship between the Enterprise Continuum and the Architecture Repository.	135
Describe the classes of information held in the Architecture Repository.	135
List the three levels of the Architecture Landscape.	136
Explain the purpose of the Standards Information Base within the Architecture Repository.	135

Table 11: *Enterprise Continuum & tools exam syllabus checklist*

Understand the Definition of Key Terms

Define the following key terms from this chapter and check your answers:

- Architecture Building Blocks
- Architecture Capability
- Architecture Continuum
- Architecture Landscape
- Architecture metamodel
- Architecture Repository
- Capability Architectures
- Common Systems Architectures
- Common Systems Solutions
- Enterprise Continuum
- Foundation Architectures
- Foundation Solutions
- Foundational Frameworks
- Governance Log
- Industry Architectures
- Industry Solutions
- Organisation-Specific Architectures
- Organisation-Specific Solutions
- Reference Library
- Segment Architectures
- Solutions Continuum
- Standards Information Base
- Strategic Architectures

Complete the Review Questions

Check your understanding of this chapter by answering the following example exam-style questions:

Q1. Which of the following are <u>not</u> true of the Enterprise Continuum?
(Select 2)

    A. The Enterprise Continuum is a repository area that can hold a set of specifications, to which architectures must conform.

    B. The Enterprise Continuum is a view of the Architecture Repository that classifies the architecture and solution artefacts as they evolve from generic architectures to organisation-specific architectures.

    C. The Enterprise Continuum is a *virtual repository* for architecture assets such as models, patterns, architecture descriptions and other artefacts.

    D. The Enterprise Continuum is part of the enterprise IT repository, which links architectural assets to other repositories containing components such as detailed designs, deployment details and service management.

    E. The Enterprise Continuum enables the classification of reusable architecture and solution assets.

Q2. Which class of architectural information held within the Architecture Repository would most likely contain adopted reference models?   (Select 1)

    A. Architecture metamodel

    B. Architecture Capability

    C. Standards Information Base

    D. Reference Library

Q3. The Enterprise Continuum comprises of which two continuums?
(Select 2)

    A. Architecture Continuum

    B. Business continuum

    C. Data continuum

    D. Technology continuum

    E. Solutions Continuum

Q4. Which of the following does the Enterprise Continuum hold in a virtual repository?
(Select 1)

    A. Just industry-reference models.

    B. All architectural assets.

    C. Just internal reusable architecture and solution assets.

    D. Just the artefacts produced during the ADM phases.

    E. Only external architecture and solution artefacts, such as industry-reference models.

Q5. Which two reference models for inclusion in the Enterprise Continuum does TOGAF provide?
(Select 2)

    A. The TOGAF Solution Architecture.

    B. The TOGAF Common Solutions Architecture.

    C. The TOGAF Foundation Architecture.

    D. The Integrated Information Infrastructure Reference Model (III-RM).

    E. The Architecture Development Method (ADM).

    F. The Solutions Integrated Base Reference Model.

Q6. Which of the following define corresponding levels of the Architecture Continuum?
(Select 4)

A. Solutions Architecture

B. Foundation Architecture

C. Data Architecture

D. Common System Architecture

E. Industry Architecture

F. Organisation-Specific Architecture

G. Business-Specific Architecture

H. Target Architecture

Q7. Which of the following gives the <u>best</u> description of a Foundation Architecture?
(Select 1)

A. A Foundation Architecture describes and guides the user-written or third-party components that form the solutions for a particular enterprise.

B. A Foundation Architecture is an architecture of building blocks and corresponding standards that supports generic services and functions on which more specific architectures and architectural components can be built.

C. A Foundation Architecture is used to address specific customer problems within a particular industry domain and to guide the integration of common systems components with industry-specific components.

D. A Foundation Architecture guides the selection and integration of specific services from the Common Systems Architectures to create an architecture useful for building solutions across a wide number of relevant domains.

Q8. Which of the following gives the <u>best</u> description of a Common Systems Architecture?
(Select 1)

A. A Common Systems Architecture describes and guides the user-written or third-party components that form the solutions for a particular enterprise.

B. A Common Systems Architecture is an architecture of building blocks and corresponding standards that supports generic services and functions to provide a foundation on which more specific architectures and architectural components can be built.

C. A Common Systems Architecture is used to address specific customer problems within a particular industry domain and to guide the integration of foundation systems components with industry-specific components.

D. A Common Systems Architecture guides the selection and integration of specific services from the Foundation Architecture to create an architecture useful for building solutions across a wide number of relevant domains.

Q9. Which of the following gives the <u>best</u> description of an Industry Architecture?
(Select 1)

A. An Industry Architecture describes and guides the user-written or third-party components that form the solutions for a particular enterprise.

B. An Industry Architecture is an architecture of building blocks and corresponding standards that supports generic services and functions to provide a foundation on which more specific architectures and architectural components can be built.

C. An Industry Architecture is used to address specific customer problems within a particular vertical domain and to guide the integration of common systems components with industry-specific components.

D. An Industry Architecture guides the selection and integration of specific services from the Foundation Architecture to create an architecture useful for building solutions across a wide number of relevant domains.

140

Q10. Which of the following gives the <u>best</u> description of an Organisation Specific Architecture?
(Select 1)

    A. An Organisation Specific Architecture describes and guides the user-written or third-party components that form the solutions for a particular enterprise.

    B. An Organisation Specific Architecture is an architecture of building blocks and corresponding standards that supports generic services and functions to provide a foundation on which more specific architectures and architectural components can be built.

    C. An Organisation Specific Architecture is used to address specific customer problems within a particular industry domain and to guide the integration of common systems components with industry-specific components.

    D. An Organisation Specific Architecture guides the selection and integration of specific services from the Foundation Architecture to create an architecture useful for building solutions across a wide number of relevant domains.

Q11. Which of the following statements <u>best</u> describe the TOGAF Architecture Repository?
(Select 3)

    A. A formal structure for terms to ensure there is consistency within the ADM and to provide guidance for organisations that wish to implement their architecture within an architectural tool.

    B. An abstract framework for understanding significant relationships among the entities of an environment and for the development of consistent standards or specifications supporting that environment.

    C. A formal taxonomy for different types of architectural asset.

    D. A framework that allows an enterprise to identify the different types of architectural assets at different levels of abstraction in the organisation.

    E. Part of the enterprise IT repository, which links architectural assets to other repositories containing components such as detailed designs, deployment details and service management.

    F. The repository that relate to the architectural organisation of business and covers the business strategy, governance, organisation and key business processes information, as well as the interaction between these concepts.

Q12. What <u>best</u> describes the purpose of the Architecture Repository?
(Select 1)

    A. A tool that can be used at the programme or portfolio level to organise and operationally-align specific change activities.

    B. A representation of a related set of concerns from a specific viewpoint to demonstrate to stakeholders their areas of interest (viewpoint) in the architecture.

    C. A process that needs to be managed and governed to ensure that all architectural considerations are made and all required deliverables are produced during each phase of the ADM.

    D. A description of a discrete business operation or activity and how IT supports that operation.

    E. A package of functionality defined to meet business needs.

    F. A physical repository that contains a framework for managing architectural work products and is a model of the physical instance of the Enterprise Continuum.

Q13. Which of the following are the six classes of architectural information held in the Architecture Repository?   (Select 6)

A. Application Architecture
B. Technology Architecture
C. Architecture metamodel
D. Architecture Capability
E. Landscape Architecture
F. Architecture Landscape
G. Standards Information Base (SIB)
H. Target Architecture
I. Reference Library
J. Governance Log

Q14. Which of the following <u>best</u> describes the architecture metamodel?
(Select 1)

A. A record of governance activity across the enterprise.
B. Templates, patterns, guidelines and other material useful in the creation of new architectures for the enterprise.
C. Details of the standards which all new architectures must comply.
D. A formal structure for architectural work products and artefacts to ensure consistency within the ADM.
E. An architectural view of the (live) building blocks in use within the organisation.
F. The parameters, structures and processes that support governance of the Architecture Repository to realise the business vision.

Q15. Which of the following <u>best</u> describes the term Architecture Capability?
(Select 1)

A. A record of governance activity across the enterprise.
B. Templates, patterns, guidelines and other material useful in the creation of new architectures for the enterprise.
C. Details of the standards with which all new architectures must comply.
D. A formal structure for architectural work products and artefacts to ensure consistency within the ADM.
E. An architectural view of the (live) building blocks in use within the organisation.
F. The parameters, structures and processes that support governance of the Architecture Repository to realise the business vision.

Q16. **Which of the following <u>best</u> describes the term Architecture Landscape?**
(Select 1)

A. A record of governance activity across the enterprise.

B. Templates, patterns, guidelines and other material useful in the creation of new architectures for the enterprise.

C. Details of the standards with which all new architectures must comply.

D. A formal structure for architectural work products and artefacts to ensure consistency within the ADM.

E. An architectural view of the (live) building blocks in use within the organisation.

F. The parameters, structures and processes that support governance of the Architecture Repository to realise the business vision.

Q17. **Which of the following <u>best</u> describes the Standards Information Base (SIB)?**
(Select 1)

A. A record of governance activity across the enterprise.

B. Templates, patterns, guidelines and other material useful in the creation of new architectures for the enterprise.

C. Details of the standards with which all new architectures must comply.

D. A formal structure for architectural work products and artefacts to ensure consistency within the ADM.

E. An architectural view of the (live) building blocks in use within the organisation.

F. The parameters, structures and processes that support governance of the Architecture Repository to realise the business vision.

Q18. **Which of the following <u>best</u> describes the Reference Library?**
(Select 1)

A. A record of governance activity across the enterprise.

B. Templates, patterns, guidelines and other material useful in the creation of new architectures for the enterprise.

C. Details of the standards with which all new architectures must comply.

D. A formal structure for architectural work products and artefacts to ensure consistency within the ADM.

E. An architectural view of the (live) building blocks in use within the organisation.

F. The parameters, structures and processes that support governance of the Architecture Repository to realise the business vision.

Q19. **Which of the following <u>best</u> describes the Governance Log?**
(Select 1)

A. A record of governance activity across the enterprise.

B. Templates, patterns, guidelines and other material useful in the creation of new architectures for the enterprise.

C. Details of the standards with which all new architectures must comply.

D. A formal structure for architectural work products and artefacts to ensure consistency within the ADM.

E. An architectural view of the (live) building blocks in use within the organisation.

F. The parameters, structures and processes that support governance of the Architecture Repository to realise the business vision.

Q20. Which of the following are the levels of granularity found in the Architecture Landscape?
(Select 3)

A. Business Architectures

B. Target Architectures

C. Capability Architectures

D. Strategic Architectures

E. Data Architectures

F. Segment Architectures

G. Technology Architectures

Q21. Which of the following <u>best</u> describes a Strategic Architecture?
(Select 1)

A. A description of a discrete business operation or activity and how IT supports that operation.

B. A summary view of the entire enterprise over a long period of time.

C. A formal, more detailed description of operating models for areas within an enterprise.

D. A highly-detailed description of the architectural approach to realise a particular solution or solution aspect.

E. An architecture of generic services and functions that provides a foundation on which more specific architectures and architectural components can be built.

F. A structure of an organisation's logical and physical data assets and data management resources.

Q22. Which of the following <u>best</u> describes a Segment Architecture?
(Select 1)

A. A description of a discrete business operation or activity and how IT supports that operation.

B. A summary view of the entire enterprise over a long period of time.

C. A formal, more detailed description of operating models for areas within an enterprise.

D. A highly-detailed description of the architectural approach to realise a particular solution or solution aspect.

E. An architecture of generic services and functions that provides a foundation on which more specific architectures and architectural components can be built.

F. A structure of an organisation's logical and physical data assets and data management resources.

Q23. Which of the following <u>best</u> describes a Capability Architecture?
(Select 1)

A. A description of a discrete business operation or activity and how IT supports that operation.

B. A summary view of the entire enterprise over a long period of time.

C. A formal, more detailed description of operating models for areas within an enterprise.

D. A highly-detailed description of the architectural approach to realise a particular solution or solution aspect.

E. An architecture of generic services and functions that provides a foundation on which more specific architectures and architectural components can be built.

F. A structure of an organisation's logical and physical data assets and data management resources.

Q24. **Which two key issues for tools standardisation does TOGAF mention?**
(Select 2)

A.   The avoidance of vendor lock-in.

B.   Using the TOGAF Architecture Repository schema to allow data sharing between tools.

C.   The choice of a single 'one size fits all' tool versus multiple 'best of breed' tools.

D.   The ability of a single tool to address all needs and at all levels of maturity.

E.   Using XML for data storage rather that a RDBMS.

Q25. **TOGAF states that managing the contents of the Enterprise Continuum requires tools that _____?**
(Select 5)

A.   Ensure that the artefacts in the Enterprise Continuum use a common and consistent terminology.

B.   Remove the need to reuse artefacts.

C.   Allow the architecture information contained in the Enterprise Continuum to be shared within the organisation.

D.   Promote the reuse of artefacts.

E.   Restrict or prevent access to the repository by stakeholders to avoid changes being made.

F.   Allow the terminology used by artefacts in the Enterprise Continuum to be defined and changed by the particular stakeholder at any given time.

G.   Allow data to be migrated between tools with no loss of context.

H.   Reduce the burden of maintaining the architecture.

I.   Address all needs and at all levels of maturity in a single tool to avoid duplication of tools.

J.   Provide stakeholders with the relevant models that reflect their areas of concern by supporting enquiries for models, views and other queries.

Review your answers

Review your answers by referring to the answers that can be found on page 183.

Further Reading and Resources

The following list provides further recommended sources of information for the areas covered by this chapter:

- TOGAF 9 Part V - *Enterprise Continuum & Tools* (Chapters 38 to 42)

This chapter covers the following exam subjects:

- Define what building blocks are, and what makes a good building block.
- Explain the distinction between Architecture Building Blocks and Solution Building Blocks.
- Explain where building blocks are defined and used within the ADM cycle.
- Describe the characteristics of an Architecture Pattern.

Building Blocks & Architecture Patterns

The purpose of this chapter of the Study Guide is to understand the concept and use of building blocks within TOGAF and the role of Architecture Patterns.

Building Blocks

A building block is a component of business, IT or architectural capability that has the following characteristics:

- It is a package of functionality defined to meet the business needs across an organisation.
- It has published interfaces to access functionality.
- It may interoperate with other building blocks.
- It may have many different implementations.

Characteristics of a Good Building Block

A good building block has the following additional characteristics:

- It considers implementation / usage and can evolve to exploit new technology and standards.
- It may be assembled from other building blocks.
- It is reusable and replaceable, with well-specified and stable interfaces.
- Its specification should be loosely coupled to its implementation, so that it can be realised in several ways without impacting on the building block specification.

Relationship between Building Blocks and Architecture

An architecture can be considered to be a composition of a set of building blocks depicted in an architectural model, and a specification of how those building blocks are connected to meet the overall requirements of a system.

The way that products and customer developments are assembled into building blocks will vary between individual architectures, and it is for each organisation to decide what arrangement of building blocks to use. By choosing good building blocks, the organisation can improve legacy system integration, interoperability and flexibility in the creation of new systems.

Relationship between Building Blocks and Services

The building blocks that make up the architecture define the services required in an enterprise-specific system and should conform to agreed standards. An architecture should need only one set of building blocks to implement the services it requires, but this does not mean there is a always a 1:1 mapping relationship between a building block and a service. A building block may define one service, more than one, or a partial service identified in the architecture.

Architecture Building Blocks and Solution Building Blocks Overview

Systems can be built from collections of buildings blocks defined at different levels of detail. Building blocks defined at the functional level, such as a RDBMS, are known as Architecture Building Blocks and are related to the Architecture Continuum. In contrast, real products or specific custom developments are known as Solutions Building Blocks. For example, a relational database would be considered an architectural building block, whilst Microsoft's SQL server 2008 or Oracle 11g could be considered a potential Solution Building Block.

Architecture Building Blocks Overview

Architecture Building Blocks consist of architecture documentation and models taken from the enterprise's Architecture Repository and are classified according to the Architecture Continuum. They are defined or selected during application of the ADM - mainly in Phases A, B, C and D.

Architecture Building Blocks are defined by the following characteristics:

- They capture architecture requirements; e.g., business, data, application and technology requirements.
- They direct and guide the development of Solution Building Blocks.
- Their functionality and attributes define clearly what functionality will be implemented.

As a minimum, Architecture Building Block specifications should contain:

- Fundamental functionality and attributes: semantic, unambiguous, including security capability and manageability.
- Details of interfaces.
- Relationship to other building blocks.
- Dependent building blocks with well-defined interfaces, functionality and named user interfaces.
- A map to business / organisational entities and policies.
- They are normally product-neutral and vendor-neutral (e.g. Relational Database, rather than Oracle 11g).

The specification and development of building blocks using the ADM is an evolutionary and iterative process.

Solution Building Blocks

Solution Building Blocks are implementations of the architectures identified in the enterprise's Architecture Continuum and may be either procured or developed. Solution Building Blocks make up the Solutions Continuum and appear in the ADM Opportunities & Solutions Phase where product-specific building blocks are considered for the first time. Solution Building Blocks define what products and components will implement the functionality and, therefore, define the implementation.

Solution Building Blocks are defined by the following characteristics:

- They define what products and components will implement the functionality.
- They define the implementation.
- They fulfil business requirements.
- They are product and/or vendor-aware (e.g. Oracle 11g, rather than Relational Database).

As a minimum, Solution Building Block specifications should contain:

- Specific functionality and attributes.
- A set of implemented interfaces.
- Details of other required Solution Building Blocks used, with further details of the functionality and names of interfaces used.
- A mapping from the Solution Building Blocks to the IT topology and operational policies.
- Specifications of shared attributes, such as security, manageability and scalability.
- Performance and configuration details.
- Design drivers and constraints, including physical architecture.
- Relationship mapping back to Architecture Building Blocks.

Building Blocks and the ADM Cycle

Building blocks can be defined at various levels of detail, depending on what phase of ADM has been reached. At early phases, a building block may simply consist of a grouping of functionality, such as a customer database and retrieval tools. A building block at this functional level is described in TOGAF as an Architecture Building Block. Later, products or developments will replace these simple definitions of functionality and the building blocks are then described by TOGAF as Solution Building Blocks.

The key phases and steps of the ADM at which building blocks are evolved and specified are summarised as follows:

- In the Architecture Vision Phase, the earliest building block definitions start as relatively abstract entities within the Architecture Vision (outline Architecture Building Blocks).
- In Phases B, C and D, building blocks within the Business, Information Systems (data / application) and Technology Architectures are evolved to a common pattern of steps (well-defined Architecture Building Blocks).
- Finally, in the Opportunities & Solutions Phase the Architecture Building Blocks become more implementation-specific as Solution Building Blocks are identified to address gaps.

Systems are built from collections of building blocks, and it is important that the interfaces to a building block are published and stable as they will need to interoperate with each other.

A Building Blocks Process Example

This example illustrates the process of how building blocks are identified and defined when executing the ADM.

Identify Building Block Scope

This stage defines what items are in scope, the boundary and the budget. It also defines the business process using use-case models, documents assumptions, and develops new requirements. A simplified set of candidate building blocks for the business process can then be built from the elements of the use-case table considered to be in scope.

Identify Building Block Requirements and Constraints

This stage builds a high-level description of the characteristics of the current system, identifies the reusable building blocks, describes the technical functionality, and identifies additional constraints. These documents provide the starting point for architectural development and list the interoperability issues that the final architecture will have to take into account. Potential reusable building blocks contained in the existing environment are identified as candidate building blocks from the Baseline Architecture.

149

Model the Architecture

In ADM Phases B, C and D, different architecture views are considered and used to build a model for the new architecture. A model of the Baseline Architecture and initial Target Architecture are developed. The candidate building blocks from the earlier stages are then considered, with some candidates becoming recommended building blocks. A set of building block specifications are then produced.

Identify Opportunities

This is the step where projects are identified, ranked, and selected to be taken forward for implementation.

Identify Building Blocks for Reuse

Diagrams showing the building blocks in a system can be used to identify or prioritise future projects. They can also be used to identify sub-sets of common functionality among applications and to pick out reusable components in the architecture. An alternative approach is to create a matrix of the building blocks used in an architecture and the applications that use them.

Architecture Patterns

An Architecture Pattern is defined as:

> *An idea that has been useful in one practical context and will probably be useful in others.*

The contents of a pattern contain:

- **Name** - a unique heading reference for the pattern.
- **Problem** - a description of the situation where the patterns is applied.
- **Context** - the existing pre-conditions where the pattern is applicable.
- **Motivation** - a description of the relevant forces and constraints.
- **Solution** - a description of the pattern details.
- **Examples** - sample applications of the pattern.
- **Rationale** - an explanation of the pattern.
- **Known uses** - known applications of the pattern in existing deployed systems.

In TOGAF, Architecture Patterns are considered to be a way of putting building blocks into context in order to describe a reusable solution for a problem. Building blocks are *what* you create, but it is the Architecture Patterns that tell you *how*, *when*, *why* and *where* to use them.

Exam Preparation Tasks

Review All the Key Topics

Review the most important topics from this chapter listed in table 12 below:

Description	Page
Define what a building block is, and explain what makes a good building block.	147
Explain the distinction between Architecture Building Blocks and Solution Building Blocks.	148
Briefly explain the use of building blocks in the ADM cycle.	149
Describe the characteristics of an Architecture Pattern.	150

Table 12: *Building blocks exam syllabus checklist*

Understand the Definition of Key Terms

Define the following key terms from this chapter and check your answers:

- Architecture Building Blocks
- Architecture Patterns
- Solution Building Blocks

Complete the review questions

Check your understanding of this chapter by answering the following example exam-style questions:

Q1. **Which of the following applies to an Architecture Building Block?**
(Select 1)

    A. It defines the functionality to be implemented.

    B. It defines the implementation.

    C. It defines what products and components will implement the functionality.

    D. It is product-aware and or vendor-aware.

Q2. **Which of the following is a characteristic of a building block?**
(Select 1)

    A. A building block is always independent and is never dependent on other building blocks.

    B. A building block defines the perspective from which a view is taken.

    C. It has published interfaces to access functionality.

    D. A building block is a representation of a system from the perspective of a related set of concerns.

Q3. **Which of the following characteristics define a good building block?**
(Select 2)

    A. It considers implementation, usage and can evolve to exploit new technology and standards.

    B. Its specification should be tightly coupled to its implementation.

    C. It is reusable, replaceable and well specified with stable interfaces.

    D. It analyses the stakeholder's concerns and documents them.

Q4. **Which of the following should an Architecture Building Block specification contain as a minimum?**
(Select 2)

    A. Details of interfaces.

    B. Relationships to other building blocks and dependencies on other building blocks.

    C. Name, problem definition, context, forces (security, robustness and reliability), solution, resulting context, examples, rationale and known uses.

    D. Details confirming that it is in accordance with future directions and strategies.

Q5. **Which of the following characteristics define Solution Building Blocks?**
(Select 2)

    A. They are implementation independent.

    B. They define the implementation.

    C. They are product-aware and or vendor-aware.

    D. They are product-aware and or vendor-independent.

Q6. **Which of the following should a Solution Building Block specification contain as a minimum?**
(Select 2)

    A. A set of implemented interfaces.

    B. Details confirming that it is in accordance with future directions and strategies.

    C. Design drivers and constraints, including physical architecture.

    D. Opportunities for infrastructure simplification.

Q7. **In TOGAF, what is an Architecture Pattern considered to be?**
(Select 1)

A. A package of functionality defined to meet the business needs across an organisation.

B. It captures architecture requirements; e.g., business, data, application and technology requirements.

C. A (potentially reusable) component of business, IT or architectural capability.

D. Information on when and why to use specific building blocks.

Review Your Answers

Review your answers by referring to the answers that can be found on page 183.

Further Reading and Resources

The following list provides further recommended sources of information for areas covered by this chapter:

- TOGAF 9 Part IV - *Architecture Content Framework*, Chapter 37 (Building Blocks)

This chapter covers the following exam subject:

- The TOGAF Technical Reference Model (TRM).

CHAPTER 13

TOGAF Technical Reference Model

The purpose of this chapter of the Study Guide is to ensure that you understand the TOGAF Technical Reference Model (TRM).

The Technical Reference Model as a Foundation Architecture

Reference models are useful because they provide a common vocabulary and structure for communication between all participants on a project. TOGAF includes the Technical Reference Model as a Foundation Architecture upon which other, more specific, architectures can be based.

A Foundation Architecture is an architecture of building blocks and corresponding standards that supports all the Common Systems Architectures and, therefore, the complete computing environment. A Foundation Architecture is positioned at the left-hand side of the Enterprise Continuum (see Figure 18 on page 130) since it is generic. The ADM explains how to develop from this generic Foundation Architecture to an enterprise-specific architecture positioned on the right-hand side of the Enterprise Continuum.

Using the TOGAF Technical Reference Model allows the architect to:

- Identify duplicate functionality and opportunities for reuse of existing building blocks.
- Identify opportunities for infrastructure simplification.
- Ensure consistent use of a capability across the enterprise.
- To identify relevant open standards.

There are two reference models in TOGAF:

1. The Technical Reference Model, discussed in this chapter.

2. The Integrated Information Infrastructure Reference Model (III-RM), discussed in the following chapter.

The Major Characteristics of a Foundation Architecture

Major characteristics of a Foundation Architecture are that it:

- Reflects general computing requirements and associated building blocks.
- Defines technology standards for implementing building blocks and provides direction for products and services.
- Reflects the function of a complete, robust computing environment that can be used as a foundation.
- Is in accordance with the organisation's future directions and strategies.
- Provides open system standards, directions and recommendations.

The TRM has two complementary components:

1. A graphical representation that provides a visual representation of the taxonomy.
2. A supporting multi-level taxonomy that defines the terminology used.

Figure 23 below shows the visual representation of the Technical Reference Model. This highlights the platform service categories together with the external environment entities, such as applications and communications infrastructure.

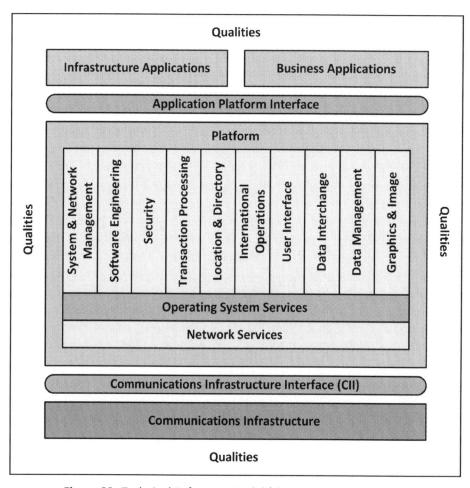

Figure 23: *Technical Reference Model (showing service categories)*

The components of the Technical Reference Model are defined as:

- **Infrastructure Applications** - provide general-purpose business functionality common to many enterprises (e.g., email).
- **Business Applications** - implement processes for a particular enterprise or vertical industry.
- **Application Platform Interface** - specifies a rigorous and complete API to ensure application portability across which all services are provided.
- **Application Platform** - the application software addresses the business requirements of the enterprise and the TOGAF Technical Reference Model defines an application platform that contains all possible services. The application platform for a specific Target Architecture will contain only the services needed to support the required functions.
- **Communications Infrastructure Interface (CII)** – is the interface between the application platform and the communications infrastructure. This is almost always a set of core services supported by IP-based networks.

- **Communications Infrastructure** - provides basic services to interconnect systems to achieve transfer of data. This component contains both hardware and software elements and hides the networks and physical communications infrastructure.
- **Qualities** - these are 'non-functional' requirements applicable across components and are shown in the diagram as a back plane behind all of the services. Service qualities would include manageability, reliability, performance, security, integrity, interoperability, scalability and portability.

The Architectural Objectives of the Technical Reference Model

The Technical Reference Model fulfils two architectural objectives:

1. **Application portability** is achieved through the application platform interface by identifying a set of services made available to application via the platform.
2. **Interoperability** is achieved through the communications infrastructure interface by identifying the communications infrastructure services that can be leveraged by the platform.

TOGAF ADM and the Technical Reference Model

The TOGAF Technical Reference Model provides a core taxonomy for, and a structured definition of, the application platform. Using TOGAF ADM is not dependent upon the use of the TOGAF Technical Reference Model or its associated taxonomy. An enterprise is free to use TOGAF Technical Reference Model as it stands, to modify and adapt the TOGAF Technical Reference Model, or even to adopt a different Technical Reference Model.

Exam Preparation Tasks

Review All the Key Topics

Review the most important topics from this chapter listed in table 13 below:

Description	Page
Explain the role of the Technical Reference Model as a Foundation Architecture.	155
Describe the major characteristics of a Foundation Architecture.	155

Table 13: *TOGAF TRM exam syllabus checklist*

Understand the Definition of Key Terms

Define the following key terms from this chapter and check your answers:

- Application Platform Interface
- Communications Infrastructure Interface
- Technical Reference Model
- Foundation Architecture

Complete the review questions

Check your understanding of this chapter by answering the following example exam-style questions:

Q1. Why are reference models useful?
(Select 1)

A. They explain how to develop from the generic Foundation Architecture to an Enterprise-Specific Architecture positioned on the right-hand side of the Enterprise Continuum.

B. They allow effective communication between all participants on a project by creating a common vocabulary and structure.

C. They all specify a rigorous and complete API to ensure application portability across which all services are provided.

D. They ensure that the Data Architecture complies with the Architecture Vision.

E. They identify duplicate functionality and opportunities for reuse of existing building blocks.

Q2. What is a Foundation Architecture?
(Select 1)

A. A rigorous and complete API to ensure application portability across which all services are provided.

B. A single Solution Building Block that supports all the enterprise's system architectures and, therefore, the complete computing environment.

C. A single Solution Building Block that supports all the Common Systems Architectures and, therefore, the complete computing environment.

D. An architecture of building blocks and corresponding standards that supports all the enterprise's systems architectures and, therefore, the complete computing environment.

E. An architecture of building blocks and corresponding standards that supports all the Common Systems Architectures and, therefore, the complete computing environment.

Q3. Which of the following does using a Technical Reference Model allow an architect to do?
(Select 4)

A. Ensure that the Data Architecture complies with the Architecture Vision.

B. Identify duplicate functionality and opportunities for reuse of existing building blocks.

C. Provides a clear path to develop the Architecture Building Blocks from the Solution Building Blocks.

D. Identify opportunities for infrastructure simplification.

E. Ensure consistent use of capability across the enterprise.

F. To ensure that the architectural change management overhead is minimised.

Q4. What are the names of the two reference models in TOGAF?
(Select 2)

A. The Technical Reference Model.

B. The Integrated IT Infrastructure Reference Model.

C. The Integrated Information Infrastructure Reference Model.

D. The Platform Infrastructure Technical Reference Model.

Q5. What are the complementary components of the Technical Reference Model?
(Select 2)

A. A Data Architecture reference model.

B. A graphic that provides a visual representation of the taxonomy.

C. A Technology Architecture reference model.

D. A platform infrastructure reference model.

E. A supporting multi-level taxonomy that defines terminology.

Q6. **What two architectural objectives does the Technical Reference Model best fulfil?**
(Select 2)

A. Platform portability is achieved through the platform interface by identifying a set of services made available to application via the platform.

B. Application portability is achieved through the application platform interface by identifying a set of services made available to application via the platform.

C. Interoperability is achieved through the communications infrastructure interface by identifying the communications infrastructure services that can be leveraged in a standard way by the platform.

D. There is consistent use of capability across the enterprise.

E. To ensure that the solution complies with the Architecture Vision.

Q7. **Which of the following are components of the Technical Reference Model?**
(Select 3)

A. Infrastructure Applications, Application Platform Interface, Business Applications and Application Platform.

B. Network infrastructure, business platform interface and application interface.

C. Physical Network Infrastructure Interface (PNII)

D. Communications Infrastructure Interface (CII) and Communications Infrastructure.

E. Qualities.

Review Your Answers

Review your answers by referring to the answers that can be found on page 183.

Further Reading and Resources

The following list provides further recommended sources of information for the areas covered by this chapter:

- TOGAF 9 Part VI: *TOGAF Reference Models*
- The TOGAF website: www.togaf.info

This chapter covers the following exam subjects:

- Boundaryless Information Flow™.
- The TOGAF Integrated Information Infrastructure Reference Model (III-RM).
- The relationship of the Integrated Information Infrastructure Reference Model to the concept of Boundaryless Information Flow.

TOGAF Integrated Information Infrastructure Reference Model

The purpose of this chapter of the Study Guide is to ensure that you understand the TOGAF Integrated Information Infrastructure Reference Model (III-RM) and the concept of Boundaryless Information Flow™.

Boundaryless Information Flow™

Boundaryless Information Flow is a trademark of *The Open Group* and is a shorthand representation of *'access to integrated information to support business process improvements'*. This represents a desired state of an enterprise's infrastructure that is specific to the business needs of the organisation.

An infrastructure that provides Boundaryless Information Flow has open standard components that provide services that combine multiple sources of information and deliver the information securely whenever and wherever it is needed, in the right context for the people or systems using that information.

The Integrated Information Infrastructure Reference Model (III-RM)

The Integrated Information Infrastructure Reference Model focuses on the application software space and is a *'Common-Systems-Architecture'* in Enterprise Continuum terms. The III-RM provides a framework to enable Boundaryless Information Flow in enterprise environments and relates to, and complements, the Technical Reference Model. The III-RM expands parts of the Technical Reference Model (business applications and infrastructure applications) and also uses some of the services defined in the Technical Reference Model. Like the TOGAF Technical Reference Model, the III-RM has two main components:

1. A taxonomy, which defines terminology and provides a coherent description of the components and conceptual structure of an integrated information infrastructure.
2. An associated graphic to aid understanding by providing a visual representation of the taxonomy and the inter-relationship of the components.

It is fundamentally an Application Architecture Reference Model that shows the application components and application services software essential for an integrated information infrastructure. It includes information provider and consumer applications, as well as brokering applications - see figure 24 on page 162:

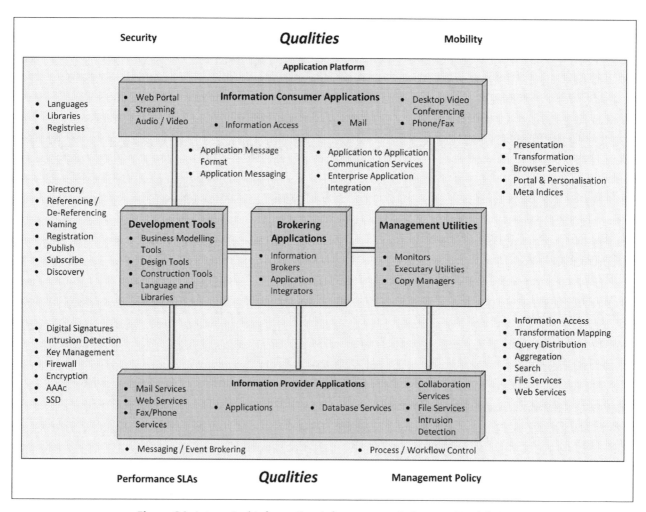

Figure 24: *Integrated Information Infrastructure Reference Model view*

The Relationship of the III-RM to Boundaryless Information Flow

Boundaryless Information Flow is essentially the challenge of providing information to the right people at the right time in a secure, reliable manner to support the core operations of the enterprise.

Organisations recognise that they need to enable people to come together in cross-functional teams so that all the skills, knowledge and expertise can be brought to bear on any specific problem or business opportunity. The aim is to provide an organisation's staff with:

- Integrated information so that multiple copies of (potentially conflicting) information are not distributed throughout different systems (i.e., to avoid multiple and inconsistent billing addresses for a customer).
- Integrated access to that information so that staff can access all the information they need, and have a right to, through one convenient interface.

The infrastructure that enables this vision is termed the *'Integrated Information Infrastructure'*. The III-RM provides insights related to customer needs for Boundaryless Information Flow in enterprise environments.

Exam Preparation Tasks

Review All the Key Topics

Review the most important topics from this chapter listed in table 14:

Description	Page
Briefly explain the basic concepts of the Integrated Information Infrastructure Reference Model.	161
Briefly explain the relationship of the Integrated Information Infrastructure Reference Model to the concept of Boundaryless Information Flow.	162

Table 14: *TOGAF Integrated Information Infrastructure Reference Model (III-RM) exam syllabus checklist*

Understand the Definition of Key Terms

Define the following key terms from this chapter and check your answers:

- Boundaryless Information Flow
- Integrated Information Infrastructure Reference Model (III-RM)

Complete the Review Questions

Check your understanding of this chapter by answering the following example exam-style questions:

Q1. Which of the following architecture domains does the Integrated Information Infrastructure Reference Model (III-RM) describe? (Select 1)

- A. Business
- B. Data
- C. Application
- D. Technology

Q2. Which of the following <u>best</u> defines the term 'Boundaryless Information Flow'? (Select 1)

- A. Boundaryless Information Flow is a buzzword of *The Open Group* and is a shorthand representation of 'access to all information from anywhere, any time to support business process improvements'.
- B. Boundaryless Information Flow is used by *The Open Group* to define the use of web services to allow 'access to integrated information to support business process improvements'.
- C. Boundaryless Information Flow is a trademark of *The Open Group* and is a shorthand representation of 'access to integrated information to support business process improvements'.
- D. Boundaryless Information Flow is a patent of *The Open Group* and is a shorthand representation of 'access to integrated information to support business process improvements'.

Q3. What are the two main parts of the Integrated Information Infrastructure Reference Model (III-RM)? (Select 2)

- A. Infrastructure applications, application platform interface, business applications, application platform.
- B. Network infrastructure, business platform interface, application interface.
- C. Qualities.
- D. A taxonomy, which defines terminology and provides a coherent description of the components and conceptual structure of an Integrated Information Infrastructure.
- E. A graphic, which provides a visual representation of the taxonomy and the inter-relationship of the components as an aid to understanding.

Q4. **Which of the following statements define the Integrated Information Infrastructure Reference Model (III-RM)?** **(Select 3)**

A. The III-RM is a reference model that focuses on the application software space and is a 'Common-Systems-Architecture' in Enterprise Continuum terms.

B. The III-RM defines a Communications Infrastructure Interface (CII) between the Application Platform and the Communications Infrastructure.

C. The III-RM defines a Communications Infrastructure that provides basic services to interconnect systems to achieve transfer of data. This component contains both hardware and software elements and hides the networks and physical communications infrastructure.

D. The III-RM provides a framework to enable Boundaryless Information Flow in enterprise environments and relates to, and complements, the TRM.

E. The III-RM expands parts of the TRM (Business Applications and Infrastructure Applications) and also uses some of the services defined in the TRM.

F. The III-RM defines qualities which are 'non-functional' requirements applicable across components. Qualities include manageability, reliability, performance, security, integrity, interoperability, scalability and portability.

Q5. **Which of the following are high-level groups for the Integrated Information Infrastructure Reference Model (III-RM)?** **(Select 5)**

A. Information Consumer Applications.

B. Application Integrators.

C. Development Tools.

D. Brokering Applications.

E. Security.

F. Language and Libraries.

G. Management Utilities.

H. Information Providing Applications.

I. Database Services.

Review Your Answers

Review your answers by referring to the answers that can be found on page 183.

Further Reading and Resources

The following list provides further recommended sources of information for areas covered by this chapter:

- TOGAF 9 Part VI - *TOGAF Reference Models*

This chapter covers the following exam subjects:

- Explaining the concept of Architecture Governance and why it is beneficial.
- Describing the main concepts that make up an Architecture Governance Framework.
- Listing the reasons for having an Architecture Board and its responsibilities.
- Explaining the role of Architecture Contracts.
- Explaining the need for, and meaning of, architecture compliance.
- Explaining the purpose of Architecture Compliance Reviews and describing the Architecture Compliance Review process.
- Explaining how the ADM can be used to establish an Architecture Capability.

CHAPTER 15

Architecture Governance

This chapter of the Study Guide is to ensure that you understand how Architecture Governance contributes to the Architecture Development Method cycle.

What is Governance?

Governance is not about overt control and strict adherence to rules. It's about ensuring that business is conducted properly to make effective use of resources to ensure sustainability of an organisation's strategic objectives at an enterprise-wide level.

Governance Characteristics

The following characteristics are used in TOGAF to highlight both the value of and the necessity for, governance as an approach to be adopted by an organisation:

Discipline

All parties will commit to adhere to procedures, processes and authority structures established by the organisation.

Transparency

All decisions and actions implemented will be available for inspection by authorised parties.

Independence

All processes and decision-making will be established to minimise or avoid conflicts of interest.

Accountability

Identifiable groups within the organisation will be authorised and accountable for their actions and decisions.

Responsibility

All parties are required to act responsibly to the organisation and its stakeholders.

Fairness

All decisions taken, processes used, and their implementation will not be allowed to create unfair advantage to any one particular party.

The Architecture Governance Framework

Architecture Governance is the method by which an Enterprise Architecture is managed and controlled. Architecture Governance includes:

- Implementing a system of controls to ensure effective introduction, implementation and evolution of architectures within the organisation by monitoring all architecture components and activities.
- Implementing a system to ensure compliance with internal and external standards and regulatory obligations.
- Establishing processes that support Architecture Governance to agreed service levels.
- Developing processes that ensure accountability to stakeholders.

The Architecture Governance strategy should establish a cross-organisational Architecture Board to oversee the implementation of the governance strategy. This body should be representative of all the key stakeholders in the architecture who are responsible for the review and maintenance of the overall architecture. Ensuring the compliance of individual projects within the Enterprise Architecture via an architecture compliance strategy is an essential aspect of Architecture Governance.

Architecture Governance should ensure that the Architecture Contracts between development partners and sponsors on the deliverables, quality and fitness-for-purpose of an architecture are used to ensure successful implementations.

The Benefits of Architecture Governance

Architecture Governance is beneficial because it:

- Links the organisation's business strategies and objectives to the IT processes and resources.
- Helps to institutionalise IT best practices and aligns with industry frameworks such as COBIT.
- Enables the organisation to take better advantage of its information, infrastructure, hardware and software assets.
- Helps to protect the underlying digital assets of the organisation.
- Supports regulatory and best practice requirements such as security, responsibility and accountability.
- Makes risks more visible to stakeholders and promotes the management of risk.

The Main Concepts that make up an Architecture Governance Framework

Implementation Governance is covered by Phase G of the TOGAF ADM where the Target Architecture is achieved through change projects. Architecture Governance covers the management and control of the development of architectures, and is supported by an Architecture Governance Framework (such as TOGAF) used to identify processes to document, communicate and effectively manage business responsibilities.

Concept Structure

The key concepts of Architecture Governance are shown in figure 25 on page 169:

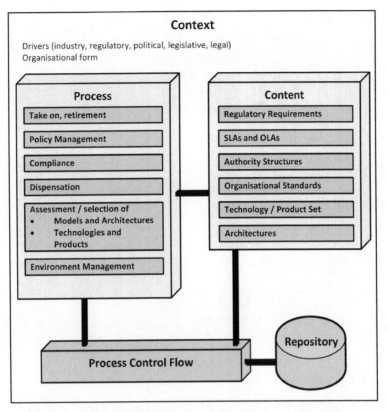

Figure 25: *Architecture Governance framework - conceptual structure*

The key to supporting the Architecture Governance initiative is achieved by splitting process and content apart. By being 'content agnostic', the framework remains flexible and allows the introduction of new governance material (such as new regulations) without unduly impacting on the processes.

Architecture Governance can be thought of as a cultural approach, with a set of related processes and owned responsibilities that ensure the integrity and effectiveness of the organisation's architectures.

Key Architecture Governance Processes

The following are the key processes:

- **Policy management** - to ensure integration with existing governance content, so that all relevant parties, documents, contracts and supporting information are managed and audited.
- **Compliance & dispensation** - to ensure stability, conformance and performance monitoring through assessments against service level agreements (SLAs), operational level agreements (OLAs), standards and regulatory requirements.
- **Monitoring & reporting** - to ensure that both the operational and service elements are managed against an agreed set of criteria.
- **Business control & environment management** - to ensure compliance with the organisation's business policies and to ensure that the repository-based environment underpinning the governance framework is effective and efficient.

Organisational Structure

Architectural Governance is the practice of managing and controlling architectures within an organisation. To achieve an effective Architecture Governance structure, the organisation requires processes, structures and capabilities (see figure 26 on page 170):

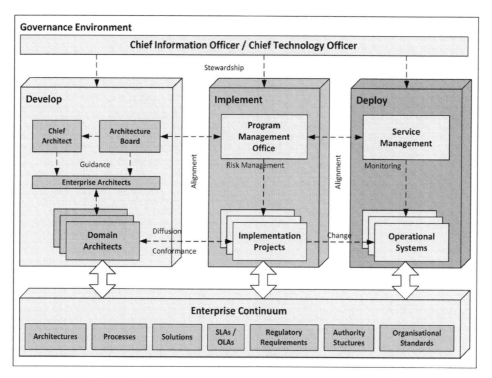

Figure 26: *Architecture Governance Framework - organisational structure*

Architectural Governance will typically consist of a global governance board, a local governance board, design authorities and supporting working parties.

The Architecture Board

Implementing an Architecture Governance strategy requires a cross-organisational Architecture Board to oversee its implementation and to ensure that any Enterprise Architecture imposed has the appropriate political backing. This Architecture Board should be made up of representatives from all the key stakeholders in the architecture, and will typically be comprised of a group of executives responsible for the review and maintenance of the overall architecture.

The costs associated with running an Architecture Board are not trivial; however, these costs can be offset by the savings that accrue as a result of preventing one-off solutions and unconstrained developments across the enterprise. The savings gained by having an Architecture Board are achieved by reducing or eliminating:

- High costs of development.
- High costs of operation and support caused by numerous run-time environments, implementation languages, interfaces and protocols.
- Low quality solutions.
- High risk projects.
- Difficulty in reusing solutions.

Responsibilities of an Architecture Board

The Architecture Board is responsible and accountable for:

- Ensuring the flexibility of Enterprise Architecture so that it is able to meet business needs and leverage new technologies.
- Improving the maturity level of architecture discipline within the organisation.
- Ensuring that the discipline of architecture-based development is adopted by the organisation.
- Enforcing architecture compliance and consistency between sub-architectures.
- Identifying reusable components and establishing reuse targets.
- Decision making with regard to changes to the architectures and proving a visible escalation capability for out-of-bounds decisions.

The Architecture Board is also responsible for operational items such as Architecture Contracts, holding regular meetings to resolve ambiguities, issues and conflicts that have been escalated, and for producing usable governance materials.

Change Requests and the Architecture Board

The Architecture Board is responsible for assessing and approving requests for change (RFCs) and for deciding if a change request should be approved or if another project in a transition architecture will resolve the issue. In some instances, a change request may drive a change in the Enterprise Architecture itself.

Architecture Contracts

Architecture Contracts are joint agreements between development partners and sponsors on the deliverables, quality, and fitness-for-purpose of an architecture that occur at various stages of the ADM. Successful implementation of these agreements is achieved through Architecture Governance by continuously monitoring the integrity, changes, decision making and audit, as well as project adherence to the principles, standards and requirements of the enterprise.

The Two Main Types of Architecture Contract

There are two distinct types of contract:

1. Those between the architecture design and development partners.
2. Those between the architectural function and the business users.

Benefits of Architecture Contracts

Successful implementation of Architecture Contracts will be delivered through effective Architecture Governance. By implementing a governed approach to the management of contracts, the following will be ensured:

- Continuous monitoring to check integrity, decision making, change management and auditing of all architecture-related activities within the organisation.
- Adherence to the principles, standards and requirements of the existing or developing architectures.
- Identification of risks associated with the architecture(s), and the mitigation and management of residual risks.
- Processes to ensure accountability, responsibility and discipline in the development and use of architectural artefacts.

- Formal understanding of the governance organisation responsible for the contract, authority and scope of the architecture.

Architecture Compliance

The TOGAF meaning for different levels of compliance is explained and shown graphically in figure 27 below:

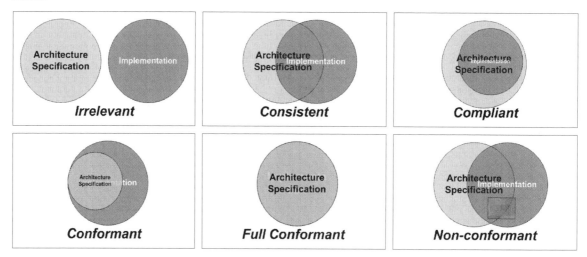

Figure 27: *Levels of architecture conformance*

Irrelevant

The implementation has no features in common with the architecture specification.

Consistent

The implementation has some features in common with the architecture specification that have been implemented in accordance with the specification. However, some other features in the architecture specification are not implemented, and the implementation has other features that are not covered by the architecture specification.

Compliant

Some features in the architecture specification are not implemented, but all the features implemented are covered by the specification and are in accordance with it.

Conformant

All the features in the architecture specification are implemented in accordance with the specification, but some other features are implemented that are not in accordance with it.

Fully Conformant

All specified features are implemented in accordance with the architecture specification, and there are no features implemented that are not covered by the specification.

Non-Conformant

This covers any of the above in which some features in the architecture specification are implemented, but not in accordance with the specification.

The Need for Architecture Compliance

Architecture Governance must ensure the compliance of individual projects within the Enterprise Architecture. To achieve this, an architecture compliance strategy should be adopted and TOGAF recommends two complementary processes:

1. The architecture team should be required to prepare a series of project architectures that form a project-specific view of the Enterprise Architecture and illustrate how the Enterprise Architecture impacts on the major projects within the organisation.
2. The IT governance function should define a formal Architecture Compliance Review process that will review the compliance of projects with the Enterprise Architecture.

To minimise the opportunity for misinterpretation of the Enterprise Architecture and to maximise commercial negotiation, the Architecture Governance function may extend beyond the role of architecture definition. This extended role may include standards selection, participating in the technology selection process, and even in the commercial relationships involved in external service provision and product purchases.

The Purpose of Architecture Compliance Reviews

The reasons for holding Architecture Compliance Reviews are:

- To identify any errors in the project architecture early on and to reduce the cost and risk of changes required later in the project lifecycle.
- To deliver the project as early as possible so that the business gets the bottom-line benefit of the architecture development faster.
- To identify and communicate significant architectural gaps to product and service providers so that they can be addressed.
- To ensure best practices for architectural work are being used on the project.
- To provide an overview of the compliance of an architecture to mandated enterprise standards.
- To identify any services that are currently application-specific but would be better provided as part of the enterprise-wide infrastructure.
- To identify where standards may require modification.
- To document strategies for collaboration and resource sharing across multiple architecture teams and projects.
- To highlight advances in technology that may benefit or impact on a project.
- To communicate to management the status of technical readiness of the project.
- To identify key criteria for procurement activities.

The Architecture Compliance Review can be used as a forum for deciding between architectural alternatives, since the decision makers typically involved in the review can steer decisions in terms of what is best for the business.

The Architecture Compliance Review Process

An Architecture Compliance Review is a process to check the compliance of a specific project against established architectural criteria, spirit and business objectives.

TOGAF describes a process, including the roles and review steps to undertake a review and deliver an assessment report, as summarised in figure 28 on page 174:

Review Process Steps	Architecture Review Co-ordinator	Lead Architect	Project Leader	Customers	Anyone
Request Architecture Review					✓
Identify Responsible Organisation	✓				
Appoint Lead Architect	✓				
Determine Review Scope (Discovery)	✓				
Tailor Checklists		✓			
Schedule Architecture Review Meetings	✓	✓			
Interview Project Principles		✓	✓	✓	
Analyse Completed Checklists		✓			
Prepare Architectural Review Report		✓			
Present Review Findings	✓	✓		✓	
Accept Review and Sign off	✓			✓	
Send out Assessment Report / Summary		✓			

Figure 28: *Architecture Compliance Review process*

Architecture Capability

Establishing a sustainable Architecture Capability within an organisation can itself be achieved by using the TOGAF ADM to architect and govern the implementation of the four domain architectures: business, data, application and technology:

1. The **Business Architecture** of the architecture practice will highlight the Architecture Governance, architecture processes, architecture organisational structure, architecture information requirements and architecture products.
2. The **Data Architecture** will define the structure of the organisation's Enterprise Continuum and the Architecture Repository.
3. The **Application Architecture** will specify the functionality and / or applications services required to enable the architecture practice to operate.
4. The **Technology Architecture** will define the infrastructure requirements and deployment in support of the architecture applications and Enterprise Continuum.

Exam Preparation Tasks

Review All the Key Topics

Review the most important topics from this chapter listed in table 15 below:

Description	Page
Briefly explain the concept of Architecture Governance.	167
Describe the main concepts that make up an Architecture Governance framework.	167
Explain why Architecture Governance is beneficial.	168
Briefly explain the need for establishing of an Architecture Board.	170
List the responsibilities of an Architecture Board.	171
Briefly explain the role of Architecture Contracts.	171
Briefly explain the meaning of architecture compliance.	172
Briefly explain the need for architecture compliance.	173
Briefly explain the purpose of Architecture Compliance Reviews.	173
Briefly describe the Architecture Compliance Review process.	173
Briefly explain how the ADM can be used to establish an Architecture Capability.	173

Table 15: *Architecture Governance exam syllabus checklist*

Understand the Definition of Key Terms

Define the following key terms from this chapter and check your answers:

- Architecture Governance
- Architecture Capability
- Architecture Contracts
- Architecture Compliance Review
- Architecture Board

Complete the Review Questions

Check your understanding of this chapter by answering the following example exam-style questions:

Q1. **The following are key Architecture Governance processes, except for _____?**
(Select 1)

A. Compliance
B. Budgetary control
C. Dispensation
D. Monitoring and reporting
E. Business control

Q2. **Which of the following best defines the characteristics of Architecture Governance?**
(Select 1)

A. Compliance, budgetary control, dispensation, monitoring, reporting & business control.
B. Discipline, transparency, independence, accountability, responsibility & fairness.
C. Compliance, transparency, dispensation, accountability & business control.
D. Identification, authentication, authorisation & accountability.

Q3. **Which of the following are included in Architecture Governance?**
(Select 5)

A. Developing processes that ensure accountability to stakeholders.

B. Ensuring that the business processes, policies and their operation deliver the business outcomes and adhere to relevant business regulation.

C. A framework to achieve the objectives set by the board, setting out the board's policies and staff's responsibilities concerning the financial affairs of the company.

D. Establishing processes that support agreed service levels.

E. Implementing a system to ensure compliance with internal and external standards and regulatory obligations.

F. Implementing a system of controls to ensure effective introduction, implementation and evolution of architectures within the organisation.

G. Defining and applying the system by which the organisation is directed and controlled.

Q4. **Which phase of the ADM covers Implementation Governance?**
(Select 1)

A. Phase A

B. Phase F

C. Phase G

D. Phase H

E. Phases A to D

F. The Preliminary Phase

Q5. **Which of the following are benefits of Architecture Governance?**
(Select 3)

A. It links the IT processes, resources and information to the organisation's business strategies and objectives.

B. It removes the need for the management of risk and makes risks less visible to stakeholders.

C. It ensures that the organisation will realise its business objectives.

D. It enables the organisation to take better advantage of its information, infrastructure and hardware / software assets.

E. It supports regulatory and best practice requirements such as security, responsibility and accountability.

F. It ensures that all IT projects will delivery on time and within budget.

Q6. **Which of the following are key Architecture Governance processes?**
(Select 4)

A. Financial control

B. Policy management

C. Compliance & dispensation

D. Residual risk mitigation

E. Monitoring & reporting

F. Business control & environment management

G. System delivery

Q7. Which answer <u>best</u> identifies who should be appointed to the Architecture Board? (Select 1)

    A. The chief architect, project manager and a business representative.

    B. Representatives from all the key stakeholders in the architecture.

    C. Anyone from the business who wishes to take part.

    D. Only senior members of the architecture practice to reduce costs.

    E. A member of each area of the organisation.

Q8. Which of the following are <u>reduced</u> or <u>eliminated</u> by having an Architecture Board? (Select 3)

    A. High costs of development.

    B. Low-quality solutions.

    C. Low-risk projects.

    D. Reuse of solutions.

    E. High costs of operation and support caused by numerous run-time environments, implementation languages, interfaces and protocols.

Q9. Which of the following are responsibilities of the Architecture Board? (Select 2)

    A. Ensuring the flexibility of Enterprise Architecture so that it is able to meet business needs and leverage new technologies.

    B. Ensuring that the discipline of architecture-based development is adopted by the organisation.

    C. Enforcing business compliance and consistency between projects.

    D. Building reusable components.

    E. Escalating all decision making, with regard to changes to the architectures, to the organisation's board of directors.

Q10. Which parties are the two types of Architecture Contracts normally between? (Select 2)

    A. A contract between the architecture practice and the business users.

    B. A contract between the architecture development team and the business users.

    C. A contract between the development team and sub-contractors.

    D. A contract between the Architecture Board and the architecture development team.

    E. A contract between the architecture practice and development partners.

Q11. Which of the following are major benefits of Architectural Governance of architectural contracts? (Select 2)

    A. Resolution of risks associated with the architecture(s) to ensure no residual risks.

    B. Continuous monitoring to check integrity, decision making, change management and auditing of all architecture-related activities within the organisation.

    C. Ensuring that all projects are delivered on time and within the agreed budget.

    D. Ensuring accountability, responsibility and discipline in the development and use of architectural artefacts.

Q12. Which of the following represents an architecture that is compliant with its architecture specification?   (Select 1)

    A.   The implementation has no features in common with the architecture specification.

    B.   Some features in the architecture specification are not implemented, but all the features implemented are covered by the specification and are in accordance with it.

    C.   All the features in the architecture specification are implemented in accordance with the specification, but some other features are implemented that are not in accordance with it.

    D.   All specified features are implemented in accordance with the architecture specification, and there are no features implemented that are not covered by the specification.

Q13. Which of the following <u>best</u> define the purpose of Architecture Compliance Reviews? (Select 4)

    A.   To ensure that the delivery projects are on schedule and will deliver the expected business benefit on the dates expected.

    B.   To identify any errors in the project architecture early on and to reduce the cost and risk of changes required later in the project lifecycle.

    C.   To ensure that the delivery projects are operating within budget constraints defined.

    D.   To provide an overview of the compliance of an architecture to mandated enterprise standards and ensure best practices for architectural work are being used on the project.

    E.   To identify any services that are currently application-specific but would be better provided as part of the enterprise-wide infrastructure.

    F.   To communicate to management the status of technical readiness of the project.

Review Your Answers

Review your answers by referring to the answers that can be found on page 183.

Further Reading and Resources

The following list provides further recommended sources of information for areas covered by this chapter:

- TOGAF 9 Part VII - Chapter 46 (Architecture Capability Framework)
- TOGAF 9 Part VII - Chapter 47 (Architecture Board)
- TOGAF 9 Part VII - Chapter 48 (Architecture Compliance)
- TOGAF 9 Part VII - Chapter 49 (Architecture Contracts)
- TOGAF 9 Part VII - Chapter 50 (Architecture Governance)

Answers to Questions

Chapter 1 - Introduction

Q1.	B	Q3.	A, B, D & E	Q5.	A, B & C
Q2.	C	Q4.	C		

Chapter 2 - Basic Concepts

Q1.	C				
Q2.	B	Q5.	A	Q9.	A & C
Q3.	B	Q6.	A & D	Q10.	D
Q4.	B	Q7.	A & D		
		Q8.	A & C		

Chapter 3 - Core Concepts

Q1.	D				
Q2.	C	Q7.	B	Q13.	B
Q3.	C	Q8.	A & D	Q14.	C & D
Q4.	B	Q9.	D	Q15.	D
Q5.	B	Q10.	A & C	Q16.	A & C
Q6.	B & D	Q11.	C & D		
		Q12.	A & C		

Chapter 4 - TOGAF Definitions

Q1.	D	Q17.	D	Q33.	D
Q2.	B	Q18.	B	Q34.	B
Q3.	D	Q19.	C	Q35.	B
Q4.	D	Q20.	A	Q36.	C
Q5.	B	Q21.	A	Q37.	C
Q6.	C & D	Q22.	C	Q38.	C
Q7.	A	Q23.	D	Q39.	C
Q8.	D	Q24.	B	Q40.	B
Q9.	B	Q25.	B	Q41.	C
Q10.	A & C	Q26.	A & D	Q42.	C
Q11.	C	Q27.	C	Q43.	D
Q12.	B	Q28.	A	Q44.	B
Q13.	A	Q29.	D	Q45.	D
Q14.	D	Q30.	B	Q46.	B
Q15.	B	Q31.	A	Q47.	D
Q16.	D	Q32.	C		

Chapter 5 - Architecture Views, Viewpoints & Stakeholders

Q1.	D	Q4.	C	Q7.	B
Q2.	A	Q5.	C		
Q3.	D	Q6.	C		

Chapter 6 - Introduction to the Architecture Development Method (ADM)

Q1.	B, D & E	Q8.	A	Q15.	A & B
Q2.	A, B, E & F	Q9.	C & G	Q16.	D
Q3.	D	Q10.	D	Q17.	F
Q4.	B	Q11.	C	Q18.	A, B & D
Q5.	E	Q12.	C, D & E	Q19.	A, C & E
Q6.	C	Q13.	A & C	Q20.	B, C & D
Q7.	A	Q14.	C		

Chapter 7 - ADM Preliminary Phase & Phases A, B, C & D

Q1. B, C, E, F, H & I
Q2. B, D, E & F
Q3. A, B, E, F & H
Q4. C
Q5. B, C & E
Q6. A, C, D, F, H & I

Q7. D, F, G, H & I
Q8. A, B, C, E & H
Q9. B, C, E, F & H
Q10. A, C & E
Q11. A & E
Q12. A, C & E

Q13. A, C & E
Q14. D
Q15. A, B, D & G
Q16. C

Chapter 8 - ADM Phases E to H & Requirements Management

Q1. B
Q2. B, C & D
Q3. D, E, F & G
Q4. A, B, E & F

Q5. F
Q6. A, C & D
Q7. B, C, D & F
Q8. A, B & E

Q9. C & E
Q10. A, B & D
Q11. A, D & E

Chapter 9 - ADM Deliverables

Q1. B
Q2. A, C, D, F & H
Q3. A, D, E & G

Q4. C
Q5. B & C
Q6. B, D, F & G

Q7. C

Chapter 10 - ADM Guidelines & Techniques

Q1. A, B, D, G & H
Q2. A
Q3. A
Q4. D
Q5. C

Q6. A
Q7. B, F & H
Q8. E
Q9. D
Q10. B

Q11. C
Q12. A, B & D
Q13. C

Chapter 11 - Enterprise Continuum & Tools

Q1.	A & D	Q10.	A	Q19.	A
Q2.	D	Q11.	C, D & E	Q20.	C, D & F
Q3.	A & E	Q12.	F	Q21.	B
Q4.	B	Q13.	C, D, E, G, I & J	Q22.	C
Q5.	C & D	Q14.	D	Q23.	D
Q6.	B, D, E & F	Q15.	F	Q24.	C & D
Q7.	B	Q16.	E	Q25.	A, C, D, H & J
Q8.	D	Q17.	C		
Q9.	C	Q18.	B		

Chapter 12 - Building Blocks & Architecture Patterns

Q1.	A	Q4.	A & B	Q7.	D
Q2.	C	Q5.	B & C		
Q3.	A & C	Q6.	A & C		

Chapter 13 - TOGAF Technical Reference Model

Q1.	B	Q4.	A & C	Q7.	A, D & E
Q2.	E	Q5.	B & E		
Q3.	B, C, D & E	Q6.	B & C		

Chapter 14 - TOGAF Integrated Information Infrastructure Reference Model

Q1.	C	Q3.	D & E	Q5.	A, C, D, G & H
Q2.	C	Q4.	A, D & E		

Chapter 15 - Architecture Governance

Q1.	B	Q6.	B, C, E & F	Q11.	B & D
Q2.	B	Q7.	B	Q12.	B
Q3.	A, B, D, E & F	Q8.	A, B & E	Q13.	B, D, E & F
Q4.	C	Q9.	A & B		
Q5.	A, D & E	Q10.	A & E		

Index

Printed in Great Britain
by Amazon.co.uk, Ltd.,
Marston Gate.